The Seeker's Guide to
7 Life-Changing Virtues

Other books in the Seeker Series include

The Seeker's Guide to the Christian Story
Mitch Finley

Living the Beatitudes Today
Bill Dodds and Michael J. Dodds, O.P.

The Seeker's Guide to Being Catholic
Mitch Finley

CHICAGO

The
Seeker's Guide

to 7 Life-
Changing
Virtues

BILL DODDS
MICHAEL J. DODDS, O.P.

Loyola Press

Chicago

 Loyola Press

3441 North Ashland Avenue
Chicago, Illinois 60657

©1999 Bill Dodds and Michael J. Dodds, O.P.

The Seeker Series *from Loyola Press provides trustworthy guides for your journey of faith. It is dedicated to the principle that asking questions is not only all right, but essential.*

Interior design by Shawn Biner

Library of Congress Cataloging-in-Publication Data

Dodds, Bill.
    The seeker's guide to 7 life-changing virtues / Bill Dodds and Michael J. Dodds.
        p. cm. — (Seeker series)
    Includes bibliographical references.
    ISBN 0-8294-1171-2 (pbk.)
    1. Virtues 2. Christian ethics—Catholic authors.
I. Dodds, Michael J. II. Title. III. Series: Seeker series (Chicago, Ill.)
BV4635.D63 1999
241'.4—dc21   98-30741
                                     CIP

Printed in the United States of America
99 00 01 02 03 / 10 9 8 7 6 5 4 3 2 1

To our sisters
Mary, Teresa, and Betsy
with love

Contents

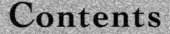

Chapter 1

Virtue and Spiritual Growth

We live in a society of spiritually hungry people. Many don't recognize the source of those hunger pangs or the way to satisfy them.

The truth is all of us want the same thing; all of us have an identical longing. Some of us don't realize what's missing from our lives. Others aren't sure how to get it. Still others have the necessary knowledge but become distracted or discouraged or simply lose their way.

"You have made us for yourself, and our hearts are restless until they rest in you," St. Augustine wrote in the fifth century. We were created to be with our Creator. Nothing else can satisfy us. Nothing else can fill us or fulfill us. Our desire to grow spiritually is nothing more—and nothing less—than our desire to grow closer to God. We want to satisfy that need while we're here on earth, even as we come to realize we can never reach that goal until we enter heaven.

But how do we encourage and nurture that growth while we're still here? We feel an emptiness, we know something is missing, and we hunt for what we think will fill it. What will fill us. What will make us happy. What will give us peace. What will make us complete. And we come up with a variety of solutions:

- Some of us gorge on "candy"—money, power, sex, drugs, or glitz and glamour—and end up with a stomachache, feeling worse than when our stomachs were empty.

- Some of us dine on "spoiled food." We grab on to some form of pseudoreligion that makes no demands on us, one that turns the words of Scripture inside out and declares us gods. We become sick and don't understand why.

- Some of walk through a "buffet line," picking and choosing what we will believe and what we won't, based solely on personal preference. We select only what tastes good right then and there and childishly pay no attention to nutrition. We accept part of what is spiritually true—the part we happen to like—and leave the rest untouched. Our body's natural resistance to illness (that is, to sin) weakens, and we seem to catch every cold and flu bug to which we're exposed.

- Finally, some of us try to live forever on "baby food." We learned of God and heaven and all the rest when we were children. But what satisfied us then no longer answers the difficult questions life is throwing at us now, the many challenges life is demanding of us. Yet instead of searching for better food, for adult food, for food that would help strengthen us to meet the needs we have today, we complain about how silly it is for anyone to eat any food, for anyone to believe in anything spiritual. We proudly confess we've outgrown that nonsense.

Few of us fall into any one of those categories completely. Most of us dabble in each category at different points in our lives. All of us can recognize people we know who accept one or the other wholeheartedly. On the other hand, it could be that through God's good graces we have begun to get a glimpse of what our life here is really all about and what really matters. We want to grow spiritually but aren't sure how to start.

This book suggests we examine seven virtues that are fundamental to our relationship with God and neighbor: faith, hope, love, prudence (wisdom), justice, fortitude (courage), and temperance (moderation or self-control). We will look at each virtue and see how it can be put into practice in our own lives.

What Is a Virtue?

It's easy to spot a virtue. Honesty is a virtue. Patience is a virtue. But it can be hard to understand the definitions of virtue because they're wrapped in abstract language. One says it's "any of the particular moral excellences considered exemplary in philosophy or theology." Another describes virtue as "a habitual, well-established readiness or disposition of one's powers directing them to some specific goodness of act." Simply put, virtue can be called a good habit: telling the truth, controlling one's temper, and so on. And a vice is the opposite: telling lies, flying off the handle, and the rest.

The Catholic Church teaches that faith, hope, and love (which are called the theological virtues) are "infused" in us by God. As the *Catechism of the Catholic Church* explains, "they have God for their origin, their motive, and their object — God known by faith, God hoped in and loved for his own sake." These three make us "capable of acting as his children and of meriting eternal life." They are the foundations of the spiritual life. As we grow in them, we become more open to God's grace, to God's blessing, to God's presence. They lead to what satisfies our most basic craving.

Prudence, justice, fortitude, and temperance are known as the cardinal (or moral) virtues. St. Ambrose, who died at the end of the fourth century, is credited with first calling them that. The term comes from the Latin *cardines,* meaning "hinges," because all the other virtues are related to, or hinge on, them. Hundreds of years earlier, these four virtues had been singled out by the Greek philosophers Plato and Aristotle and by the Roman orator and philosopher Cicero.

As the *Catechism* notes, prudence, justice, fortitude, and temperance are praised under other names in many passages of Scripture, and they "play a pivotal role" in our lives. "All the others [the human virtues] are grouped around them." They are "acquired by human effort" and "are the fruit and seed of morally good acts."

Getting into Shape

Just as there's no book that leads to instant wealth and no device that results in instant peak physical conditioning (despite what infomercials claim), a focus on the theological and cardinal virtues isn't some get-spiritually-fit-quick scheme. The *Catechism* makes that clear: "The moral virtues grow through education, deliberate acts, and perseverance in struggle." A virtuous life doesn't happen by itself.

Still, it might be helpful to compare spiritual growth to a medically sound and well-balanced program designed to get a person in shape physically. The person who only lifts weights will build up his strength but not his endurance. The one who concentrates on aerobic training but doesn't eat sensibly is going to be disappointed when her progress is so slow. A third who continues to smoke or drink too much or not get enough rest isn't going to reach top physical form.

We all know this. We've come to understand that physical fitness is like an engine that only runs correctly if all the parts are in working order. What we may not realize is that, to a large extent, the same is true for spiritual growth. We may not even be aware that it has parts or that one way to identify, or label, those parts is to refer to them as the theological and cardinal virtues.

As with any comparison, this one is not perfect, but it is a way of breaking down spiritual growth into basic components. Doing that can give us the opportunity to examine them and see how we can grow stronger in each. This may be the first time we've considered the relationship among these seven virtues, the role each can play in our life, and how, together, they shape our spirituality.

It's in this spirit that this book is written. It does not offer instant answers or promise success in only a matter of days. Rather, it presents just a taste of the vast wealth of spiritual wisdom that is a part of the church's tradition and heritage. And it encourages each of us to see how these seven virtues truly are the keys to a deeper, richer spirituality.

Faith

In One Life

Dorothy Day's life isn't quite a riches-to-rags story. It's more a middle-class-to-voluntary-poverty one. She was the cofounder of the Catholic Worker movement, known for its service to the poor and its demand for social justice.

In her young adulthood, Day (1897–1980) was a radical socialist writer who hung out —and tossed back drinks—with some of the sharpest minds on the American scene, including the playwright Eugene O'Neill. It was, at best, an agnostic crowd that scoffed at religion, calling it "the opiate of the people."

Day had her share of love affairs. The first, when she was twenty-one, ended after an abortion. The second led to marriage, but the couple divorced in less than a year. A third resulted in her only child, born out of wedlock. Her common-law husband left them when she had the infant girl baptized and she herself joined the Catholic Church.

In her many autobiographical writings, Day described how faith led her into the church and kept her there, even when she strongly disagreed with some of the things she saw happening in the name of religion. Never one to mince words or sugarcoat her opinion, she once wrote of the church: "Though she is a harlot at times, she is our Mother."

For her, Christianity was the Sermon on the Mount (Matthew 5–7). No more, no less. It was loving God totally and showing it by love of neighbor. That's the cornerstone of the Catholic Worker movement, begun in 1933. Its members believe serving the poor is serving Christ.

In the introduction to her autobiography, *The Long Loneliness*, Day quoted the character Kirilov from Dostoyevsky's novel *The Possessed:* "All my life I have been haunted by God." She continued, "This must indeed be so, as former friends and comrades have said this of me." But it wasn't that she had been raised in a religious home. "How much did I hear of religion as a child? Very little, and yet my heart leaped when I heard the name of God. I do believe every soul has a tendency toward God."

As a child, Day said, she and her siblings didn't search for God. "We took Him for granted." Evening prayer was short and simple. Religion, like sex, wasn't discussed. "It was immodest to talk of either. People were uncomfortable and embarrassed in talking about God."

Day recalled a rainy afternoon spent reading the Bible and being impressed with a neighbor girl who took her to a Protestant Sunday school and church. "I began to experience piety," she wrote, "in the sense of the sweetness of faith. I believed, but I did not know what I believed." And, she added, "I became disgustingly, proudly pious."

Another time a Catholic neighbor spoke to Day about the life of a saint. Years later, Day couldn't recall which: "I only remember my feeling of lofty enthusiasm, and how my heart almost burst with desire to take part in such a high endeavor." Referring to a verse from the Psalms, "Enlarge Thou my heart, O Lord, that Thou mayst enter it," she added, "This was one of those occasions when my small heart was enlarged and I could feel it swelling in love and gratitude to such a good God." But her spirituality was hardly mature. Day and her sister began "to practice being saints—it was a game to us."

Throughout her youth and adolescence, "I believed," Day wrote. So "it was hard to see how I could fling my convictions from me a few years later." But she did, for a time. Still, even then, during her college and early working years, she couldn't help but spot kernels of faith. "The Russian writers appealed to me. . . . Both Dostoyevsky and Tolstoy made me cling to a faith in God, and yet I could not endure feeling an alien in it. I felt that my faith had nothing in common with that of Christians around me."

When a college professor she admired talked of religion as a crutch for the weak, she "felt for the first time that [it] was something that I must ruthlessly cut out of my life. . . . I felt that I must turn from it as from a drug." Her decision, she said, was "a conscious and deliberate process."

Now seventeen and on her own, she was "divorced from my family, from all security, even from God." She felt reckless and rejoiced in that sense of danger. For her, Christ was "two thousand years dead," and "new prophets had risen up in His place." Among them were those advocating socialism.

It was the theories of Marx, not the parables of Jesus, that led Day to begin protesting the injustice she saw all around her. And it was this protesting that landed her in jail. During her short stay, the protesters started a hunger strike. "The hunger was not so bad," she wrote. "It was the dark and the cold."

She began asking for a Bible, and when one was finally given to her, she "read it with the sense of coming back to something in my childhood that I had lost." But even then, her "pride was fighting on." She did not want to turn to God "in defeat and sorrow." She didn't want to depend on him. "I tried to persuade myself that I was reading for literary enjoyment," Day recalled. "But the words kept echoing in my heart. I prayed and did not know that I prayed."

After that she began to lead, in essence, a double life. When Eugene O'Neill recited Francis Thompson's poem "The Hound of Heaven" in the smoky, boozy back room of a New York saloon, "the idea of this pursuit fascinated me." The inevitability of the poem's outcome made Day "feel that sooner or later I would have to pause in the mad rush of living and remember my first beginning and my last end."

Many mornings, after having spent all night in taverns or at dances, Day went to early morning Mass. She "knelt in the back of the church, not knowing what was going on at the altar, but warmed and comforted by the lights and silence, the kneeling people and the atmosphere of worship." There she prayed by "blind instinct." She was not conscious of praying but chose to go. "I put myself there in the atmosphere of prayer," she stressed, certain that "it was an act of the will." Always extremely bright, well read, and analytical, she came to realize that "I would have to stop to think, to question my own position. . . . What were we here for, what were we doing, what was the meaning of our lives?"

Even as Day got older and attended services with Catholic friends, she still felt like an outsider. By reading books written by converts and noticing that the Catholic Church in America was in large part an immigrant church, a workers' church, she began to feel more at home there.

At the same time, Day's personal life continued to be in shambles until she fell in love with the man who was to become her common-law husband. She became pregnant. Her career had met with success. The film rights for a roughly autobiographical novel she had written had sold for five thousand dollars. She bought a small house, not much more than a shack, on the beach at Staten Island.

There she was surprised to discover she was praying daily. She didn't fall on her knees but took long walks along the shore. She was concerned that perhaps she turned to prayer because she was lonely and unhappy. But she was neither. She prayed because she was happy and content. She wanted to thank God, so she prayed throughout the day. Years later she admitted, "It is so hard to say how this delight in prayer grew in me."

She began attending Sunday Mass regularly but could not talk about religion with her partner. A wall separated them when it came to this issue. His love of nature was drawing her to the faith, but he did not believe. In fact, she "always felt it was life with him that brought me natural happiness, that brought me to God." His love of creation led Day to the Creator. Still, she could see that "love between man and woman was incomplete without love of God."

She wrote, "God is the Creator, and the very fact that we were begetting a child made me have a sense that we were made in the image and likeness of God, co-creators with him." As the months passed, Day "knew that I was going to have my child baptized, cost what it may." She felt it was the greatest thing she could do for her child. But for herself, she "prayed for the gift of faith. I was sure, yet not sure." She held off deciding.

Becoming a Catholic would mean becoming a single parent. Her partner "would have nothing to do with religion or with me if I embraced it." Day saw it as choosing him or choosing God. And it wasn't that family life or sexual intimacy was wrong or bad. Each could be just the opposite; each could be a "sample of heaven."

"The very sexual act itself was used again and again in Scripture as a figure of the beatific vision," Day wrote. "It was not because I was tired of sex, satiated, disillusioned, that I turned to God. . . . It was because through a whole love, both physical and spiritual, I came to know God."

Day's daughter was born and baptized. A short time later Day, too, joined the church, and as she had expected, her partner walked away. She didn't regret her decision, but her life was not suddenly easy or problem free. In faith, she came to cofound the Catholic Worker movement; to study, learn, and live the social teachings of the church; to stand out nationally as a radical Catholic and a fierce pacifist; to privately accept the vows of poverty and chastity; and to sharply criticize church members who she thought needed criticizing, without ever losing her love for them and for the church they shared.

In faith, through faith, she found God.

"I found Him at last through joy and thanksgiving, not through sorrow," Day wrote in *From Union Square to Rome*. "Yet how can I can say that? . . . Better let it be said that I found Him through His poor, and in a moment of joy I turned to him."

In Scripture

The Bible, with the words that "kept echoing" in Dorothy Day's heart, is nothing if not the story of faith.

In the Old Testament, the chosen people believe God has revealed himself to them and has promised to send them the Messiah. In the New Testament, his people recognize and acknowledge that Jesus is the fulfillment of that promise. In both the Old and New Testaments, faith begins as a free gift of God who reveals himself to his people. In both, it will put demands on those who accept that gift. Their lives will never be the same again.

In the Old Testament, two Hebrew root words express faith. *'Aman* means something is certain. It's strong and solid. *Batah* means the act of believing, of trusting. The first sounds familiar because we use a version of it frequently today. At the end of a prayer, our "amen" means "Yes, I believe that." In the Old Testament, saying "amen" was like signing your name to the contract God had offered. (Deuteronomy 27:15–26 sounds like a revival meeting, with Moses urging the crowd, "All the people shall say, 'Amen!'" And in Revelation 3:14, Jesus is called "the Amen.")

Batah adds to this notion of complete trust in Yahweh the idea of getting up and doing something about it. It contains a spark of hope; in the Psalms it's used about a hundred times to indicate "believe," "trust," or "hope." Faith, to the Hebrews then, meant that combination of believing what God had revealed and trusting and hoping in what he had promised even when those promises seemed far-fetched at best.

Take Abraham, for example, whose faith in Yahweh remained firmly grounded even as his life was turned upside down. The story of Abram—as he was called before he and God entered into an agreement—begins at the end of the eleventh chapter of Genesis. In faith, Abraham does what the Lord asks of him even though what God says is hard to believe. Put another way, as Genesis 22:1 simply states, "God tested Abraham."

God tells Abraham to abandon the secure life he had established and become a nomad. He promises that Abraham will be "the ancestor of a multitude of nations," which seems unlikely since Abraham, then an old man, and his elderly wife, Sarah, have no children. Then—wonder of wonders—Sarah bears a son, Isaac, and Yahweh tells Abraham to sacrifice, meaning kill, the lad.

We know how the story ends: at the last moment, an angel of the Lord calls to Abraham and tells him the boy does not have to die (Genesis 22:11–12). Abraham has passed the ultimate test. He would not have spared his only child. He believes completely in Yahweh, and because of this faith, God says, "I will indeed bless you, and I will make your offspring as numerous as the stars in heaven and as the sand on the seashore." Abraham is held up as the model for generation upon generation. Here is someone who had faith in God. This is how he lived that faith, willing to pay any price that was asked of him because he relied on God alone.

In later times, that was what was expected of the king of Israel. Psalm 20 says it isn't horses or chariots that make him strong or bring victories in battle. Rather, "our pride [that is, faith] is in the name of the Lord."

But that's not to say the descendants of Abraham never lost faith, never failed to live out their faith. Just as the Old Testament is peppered with the stories of those who were faithful to Yahweh and to the covenant, it's riddled with those who did not believe and who turned their back on that agreement. And it wasn't just the leaders who broke the contract but also the people themselves.

During those times, it was the prophets who courageously spoke up and pointed out where the leaders and people alike were failing to keep the sacred covenant. They boldly showed how the Israelites' lack of faith in God's promise, their lack of commitment to do what God had asked of them (live according to his commandments) was causing them incredible suffering. It was when they put their faith in horses, in chariots, in anything other than the Lord that they failed to be victorious. Then their enemies overran them and took them captive.

That's what Isaiah was saying. It was what he lived. Pay attention, Israel! Here is how you have gotten off track: you aren't being faithful. And remember where that track leads—to the Messiah. But if an entire nation had spent centuries looking for the coming of this Savior, why didn't they all recognize him when he appeared? Faith . . . or, rather, the lack of it.

The New Testament uses the Greek words *pisteuein* and *pistis* for "believe" and "faith." In its classical sense, the verb *pisteuein* meant to trust in, to show confidence, and to accept as true. The noun *pistis* meant assurance, confidence, and belief. Faith, in the New Testament, included the belief that what had been promised in the Old was now fulfilled. That was a theme the evangelists repeated time and again. And now faith includes conversion. It's what John the Baptist preached. Turn away from everything contrary to God and turn toward God, which now means turn toward Jesus. To believe in God now means to believe in Jesus.

How do people demonstrate that faith? In the first three Gospels, the synoptics, it was often by their confidence. Often people had to have confidence in Jesus before he performed a miracle for them. Sometimes, though, he first performed the miracle, and that awakened faith. In any case, faith doesn't make the miracle happen. Rather, Christ can make faith a condition for his performing that miracle, for his using his divine power.

Then, too, faith is what unlocks the mystery of Jesus' words. It is the key to his message. A crowd may hear him speak, but only a handful understand. Why? Because of their faith in God. For those who lack faith, his words are only confusing or perhaps even amusing. In addition, faith, in the Gospels, means choosing Christ. Being with him. Accepting that he is, indeed, the promised one, the Messiah.

None of this means faith is something that's created by the believer himself or herself. It is a grace. Opening oneself to God and his Son, is opening oneself to the gift of faith. When Peter says Jesus is the Lord, Christ answers that it was the Father in heaven who has revealed this to him (Matthew 16:17). Peter didn't figure it out because he was smart. (The first pope was known for his boldness rather than his brains.) And, in fact, Jesus thanks the Father "because you have hidden these things from the wise and the intelligent and have revealed them to infants" (Matthew 11:25).

The Gospels also teach that faith is necessary to be Jesus' disciple. To have faith in him means to leave everything behind to follow him. Nothing is more important than that relationship and living out the duties it entails (loving God and serving others).

As many have observed, faith is at the very heart of Paul's writing. It's a theme he expounds on and examines in detail. His view is spelled out in Romans 10:4–17. Faith in Christ is necessary for salvation. Faith is a free gift from God. To be saved, one needs that gift. By that faith, not by an individual's deeds, one becomes just, one becomes holy. Nevertheless, faith is not passive. It demands action. It demands that we live in accord with what God wants.

The letter to the Hebrews contains the most familiar description of faith: "Now faith is the assurance of things hoped for, the conviction of things not seen" (Hebrews 11:1).

As in the Old Testament, faith is linked to hope. Faith allows a person to believe even when he or she has not seen. Faith makes possible the acceptance of the Good News: Christ the Son of God was born, died, rose from the dead, and ascended into heaven. That faith, that belief in Jesus, the evangelist John notes, makes it possible to begin to experience the kingdom of God here on earth because "whoever believes in the Son has eternal life" (John 3:36). And Jesus promises that he "will raise them up on the last day" (John 6:40).

Down through the Ages

It's hardly surprising that those who immediately came after the apostles—what we might call the second generation of Christianity—continued to write and preach about faith.

The apostolic fathers, as the writers of the first and second centuries are known, didn't sit down and try to come up with a neat and tidy theological explanation of this virtue. They saw their task as encouraging Christians to hang on to the faith despite difficulties and to grow in that faith. Certainly the best way they did that was to live the faith themselves and die for it.

One of the apostolic fathers was Ignatius of Antioch. He's credited with writing seven letters (epistles) that show, in part, the close relationship between faith and love. Over time a popular, but purely speculative, legend arose that Ignatius was the child whom Jesus called to his side and used as an example of humility. When the apostles asked Christ who the greatest in the kingdom of heaven was, he drew Ignatius close and said whoever humbled himself like this little one held the top spot there (Matthew 18:1–5).

That's only a tradition; now scholars say Ignatius was born in the year 35 and died around 107. For forty years, he was the bishop of Antioch, which is in Syria. He was the second successor of St. Peter there. Ignatius was arrested during the persecution of Emperor Trajan and sent to Rome. It's said that wherever the ship he was on came into port, along the coast of Asia Minor and then Greece, crowds of Christians were there to greet him. But that's not to say his captors treated him well; they didn't.

During this time, Ignatius wrote his seven letters to church communities in various locations. He did it in the same way that Paul wrote to the people of Corinth, Galatia, and so on. His style reads like Scripture, too, which only makes sense. It was the way people of that time wrote.

What do his letters say about faith in Christ? What did he say about belief as he sailed to what he had to know was certain death because of the faith he professed? In his epistle to the Ephesians he wrote, "If like Paul, you possess that faith and love toward Christ which are the beginning and end of life," then "none of the devices of the devil shall be hidden from you." With faith and love, we see clearly. We aren't deceived by what we might call Satan's smoke and mirrors.

"The beginning of life is faith, and the end is love," he continued. "And these two being inseparably connected together, do perfect the man of God; while all other things which are requisite to a holy life follow after them."

If we want to be holy, we begin with faith, which leads to love. With love, everything we need to be holy, to grow spiritually, will come.

"No man making a profession of faith ought to sin, nor one possessed of love to hate his brother," the bishop wrote. "For He [Jesus] that said, 'You shall love the Lord your God,' said also 'and your neighbor as yourself.' Those that profess themselves to be Christ's are known not only by what they say but by what they practice. 'For the tree is known by its fruit'" (Matthew 12:33).

The virtue of faith must be lived, even if it leads to persecution and death. The "Martyrdom of Ignatius" tells how he died. Written by companions who came with him to Rome, it shows how Ignatius welcomed the opportunity to join the apostles in giving up his life for Christ.

Ignatius and the others arrived in Rome on December 20, the last day for the public "games." He was led to the amphitheater and killed by lions in the arena. In gruesome detail, the account notes that "only the harder portions of his holy remains were left, which were conveyed to Antioch and wrapped in linen, as an inestimable treasure left to the holy Church by the grace which was in the martyr." This grace was faith. It was, as he had testified to Trajan before the emperor condemned him to death, "Christ within his breast."

Almost a thousand years later, the church was at a point—and Christian scholarship had developed to a point—where the matter of faith could be examined from a more philosophical angle. That was when St. Anselm (1033–1109), an Italian Benedictine who was archbishop of Canterbury, coined his definition of theology: "faith seeking understanding." He used that phrase in a work titled *Proslogium,* meaning "a discourse." Its accompanying piece was *Monologium,* meaning "a soliloquy."

Anselm explored the relationship between faith and reason. His two works were written "in the person of one who strives to lift his mind to the contemplation of God, and seeks to understand what he believes."

He wrote, "I long to understand in some degree thy [God's] truth, which my heart believes and loves. For I do not seek to understand that I may believe, but I believe in order to understand. For this also I believe—that unless I believed, I should not understand."

In other words, to start out saying "I'll believe this and I'll have faith in God only after I'm able to understand it" means never getting anywhere. If we want to understand God better, by which we mean getting to know him better, we have to believe first.

Why bother? Because, Anselm said, that's why we were created. Through sin, we've lost sight of God. Through faith, we can begin to see once more. And heaven, of course, is seeing him completely. It's the "beatific vision." (*Beatific* means not just blessed but happy.)

We "hunger" for that vision, he wrote, and that's why we seek God. And we need God to seek God. "Teach me to seek thee, and reveal thyself to me, when I seek thee," he prayed, "for I cannot seek thee, except thou teach me, nor find thee, except thou reveal thyself."

We need God to find God.

St. Anselm continued, "If one says he believes *in* it [a Supreme Being], he apparently shows clearly enough both that, through the faith he professes, he strives for that Supreme Being, and that he believes those things which are proper to this aim."

Faith is continually working toward God; here on earth, we never arrive. Faith is living a life that moves a person in that direction. It is living up to his or her part of the covenant by loving God wholeheartedly and loving neighbor as self. Faith is submitting oneself to the Word of God in Scripture and in Tradition (what the Catholic Church teaches).

At the time of the Reformation, Martin Luther (1483–1546) took issue with the idea that faith could be "living" or "dead" and argued that "faith justifies us apart from any works." It is faith that saves us, he said, not anything we do, not our "works."

"Justification by faith" was at the core of Luther's teaching, though he did maintain that "we must not draw the conclusion that we have no need to do any good works." It was an issue that would be addressed by the bishops at the Council of Trent (1545–63) and examined and argued from then on.

Simply put, the Lutheran perspective is that works proceed from faith but are not meritorious. They don't help us get into heaven. We don't get to heaven by doing. The Catholic teaching is that, because God's grace has made it so, our works *are* meritorious but are themselves a gift from God.

In recent times, C. S. Lewis (1898–1963) joined those who said, in effect, the distinction wasn't worth losing one's faith over. "Christians have often disputed as to whether what leads the Christian home is good actions, or Faith in Christ," he wrote in *Mere Christianity*. "I have no right really to speak on such a difficult question, but it does seem to me like asking which blade in a pair of scissors is most necessary."

Faith has to be more than giving into one's "moods," Lewis maintained. "For moods will change, whatever view your reason takes. I know that by experience. Now that I am Christian I do have moods in which the whole thing looks very improbable; but when I was an atheist I had moods in which Christianity looked terribly probable."

That's why, he wrote, "faith is such a necessary virtue: unless you teach your moods 'where to get off,' you can never be either a sound Christian or even a sound atheist, just a creature dithering to and fro, with its beliefs really dependent on the weather and the state of its digestion."

Daily prayers, religious reading, and church attendance are "necessary parts of the Christian life," he said, because "we have to be reminded of what we believe." He added, "If you examined a hundred people who had lost their faith in Christianity, I wonder how many of them would turn out to have been reasoned out of it by honest argument? Do not most people simply drift away?"

At the Second Vatican Council (1962–65), the Catholic bishops didn't consider just those who drift away from the Christian faith but those who have never been exposed to it, have never heard or understood the Good News. They wrote of those who are religious but sincerely place their faith in a non-Christian religion and those who seem to have no "faith" in the traditional sense.

In their Decree on Ecumenism, they taught that "faith, hope and charity can exist outside the visible boundaries of the Catholic Church." Their Decree on the Church's Missionary Activity asserted that "God in ways known to himself can lead those inculpably ignorant of the gospel to that faith without which it is impossible to please him."

Our faith in an infinite God assures us we cannot claim limits on how the Creator reveals himself to all his children and calls each one home to him.

For Us Today

It's impossible not to have faith in *something*. Christians believe in Jesus. Jews put their faith in Yahweh. Buddhists trust Buddha. Muslims rely on Allah.

Even those who are nonreligious or nominally religious have beliefs. The secular humanist believes in humankind. The atheist believes there is no God. The agnostic believes the existence of God cannot be proved or disproved. Even the person who believes chaos and random chance govern existence believes in chaos and random chance. As a novelty T-shirt proclaims, "Everyone believes in something. I believe I'll have another beer."

But what is the difference between religious faith and any other belief? What's special about religious faith? What singles it out? Belief always means putting our trust in someone else about something we don't know or can't know for ourselves. For example, we may live on the West Coast but believe it is snowing in Chicago because we trust the weather reporters. We have religious faith when the "someone" in whom we place our trust—in whose authority we have confidence—is God. We don't just believe that God exists. We don't just believe in a fact or in a statement. We believe God, who reveals himself to us in his Word and in all creation.

Belief is personal; it implies a personal relationship. We believe, we put our trust in, we rely on the three Persons of the one God who reveal themselves to us in the coming of the Son and the gift of the Holy Spirit.

If our faith is genuine, it blossoms into action. It's sometimes tempting to think that faith is like a single question on a true-or-false quiz. "I have faith." True. "I have faith." False. But it isn't that way. The virtue of faith is a take-home exam. The answer is not so much what we say but what we do. Our words count for very little; our actions, a great deal.

But maybe we're getting ahead of ourselves here. Why would we even want this religious virtue? Can't we get along fine without it?

We want it whether we know we do or not because (whether we know it or not) we want God. We want to be happy. Every human being wants that. Crudely put, we're like cars that run on high-octane gas. There's no way that what the world offers (money, power, fame, and the rest) is more than simple, cheap, and even contaminated low-octane stuff. We can get around a bit on that, but our engine never really runs right. There's problem after problem.

True happiness is heaven. It is seeing God. That taste of heaven can begin here on earth. Through faith, God reveals himself to us. In faith, we move closer to him. So faith is not just static (knowing "the facts" about God); it's personal (putting us in a relationship with God) and dynamic (drawing us into the very life of God).

Faith is where we begin. It leads us through all the other virtues to God himself. But *how* do we begin? It sounds like a catch-22. We get faith by asking for it, but we need faith to ask. What we may lose sight of is that God gives us both. He gives us the faith to ask for faith. And when we ask, he gives us more. We become better at believing by believing, just as we become better at running by running. Better at cooking by cooking. Better at listening by listening.

This isn't "which came first, the chicken or the egg?" God provides both. And he also drops hints, not unlike a mother playing hide-and-seek with a small child. She makes a little noise now and again to help her son or daughter find her.

There are moments and experiences in our lives when we feel ourselves turning to God.

Sometimes it's when we're incredibly happy or see clearly his handiwork in nature. We want to thank the Creator. Sometimes it's when we're terribly frightened or sad or lonely. We find ourselves in the "valley of the shadow of death," and we sigh with relief when we spot the Lord, our shepherd, there too.

That's not to say we have to know God well to turn to him. Or that we have to understand him before we can have faith. We are incapable of understanding him. We cannot reason our way to faith. No matter how bright we are, it's a matter of, at some point, accepting him "on faith."

But we don't have to start there, anymore than to start a diet or exercise program we have to fully understand the relationship between caloric intake and metabolic rate. We don't even have to believe the program will work. We can profess just the opposite. That doesn't matter. *As long as we follow the program,* it works.

That's how it is with faith. If we say to God "I don't believe in you and I refuse to pray," we are already talking to God. We are demonstrating belief in God's existence. And we are praying.

It takes no more than that. Like a tiny seed that falls in a sidewalk crack, faith can take root and grow. The seed needs soil, moisture, and light, but not much of any of them. Faith is the same. Our day-to-day life is the soil, to which is added moisture (hard times) and light (good times). But what makes it grow? God! In the same way that scientists cannot really explain why a seed grows, saints (theologians and the church) will never fully explain faith. Our lives, physically and spiritually, will always include mystery. But science can tell us how to promote healthy growth in plants, and saints can do the same with faith.

Faith is not a light switch, either off or on. It's a dimmer switch, but a strange sort of dimmer switch since the dimness depends on, and comes from, us. We are free. We can say no. We can shut out God's light. But the brightness comes from God: "God is light and in him is no darkness" (1 John 1:5).

At the same time, God wants us to shine. He made us to shine in his image: "You are the light of the world. . . . Let your light shine before others, so that they may see your good works and give glory to your Father in heaven" (Matthew 5:14–16).

How do we get brighter? How do we grow into a stronger plant? How do we increase that kernel of faith that we sometimes realize is within ourselves? We put that faith into action. In the beginning, that may be a halfhearted effort. We pray but don't put much stock in prayer. We show kindness to someone but claim it's simply a humanitarian deed, nothing religious. Like the father who asked Jesus to cure his sick son, we pray, "I believe; help my unbelief!" (Mark 9:24).

Step by step, prayer by prayer, deed by deed, we begin to put more heart, more of ourselves, into the effort. Degree by degree we are converted, in the true sense of the word. We turn toward God, but that doesn't mean we turn away from the world. Rather, we become better at seeing God in the world and at seeing the world as God sees it. We get better at seeing him in our fellow human beings and at realizing, and being able to admit, that he is within us.

Paradoxically, the more faith we have, the more we want. The more we live that faith, the more we want to live it—and the more inadequate we feel in our ability to live it. But, at the same time, we have more confidence that God will give us whatever we need to live that faith. Knowing that we will fall short of our abilities, we come to better appreciate and rely more fully on his mercy.

In the same way, step by step, prayer by prayer that is not prayed, deed by deed that is not done, we can let faith grow dim. We can let it wither. God allows that to happen, but we choose to make it so. We can become distracted by what the world has to offer. We can become enticed by the allure of evil. (Evil is always attractive at first glance. If it weren't, who would even consider it?) We can stumble over our own pride. We can get weighed down by our fear.

We can be like the apostle Peter when he saw Christ walking on the water (Matthew 14:22–33). We step out of the boat and start to head toward Jesus. Then we notice how strong the wind is, and doubt floods our mind and heart. We feel ourselves slipping into the cold, black water.

Faith is walking on the water in spite of the wind. It is continuing to make our way toward Jesus despite the cold, black water lapping at our feet. It is — when fear wins out and we start to go under — crying aloud, as Peter did, "Lord, save me!"

Matthew tells us that "Jesus immediately reached out his hand and caught [Peter], saying to him, 'You of little faith, why did you doubt?'" It's a gentle admonition, not words of condemnation.

He didn't turn his back on Peter. He never will on us.

To Read More about It

Dorothy Day, *The Long Loneliness: An Autobiography* (San Francisco: Harper and Row, 1981).

Fyodor Dostoyevsky, *The Possessed*, trans. Andrew R. MacAndrew (New York: Signet Classic, 1991).

Avery Dulles, S.J., *The Assurance of Things Hoped For: A Theology of Christian Faith* (New York and Oxford: Oxford University Press, 1994).

C. S. Lewis, *Mere Christianity* (New York: Macmillan, 1952).

Francis Thompson, "The Hound of Heaven" in *The Treasury of Catholic Wisdom*, ed. John A. Hardon, S.J. (San Francisco: Ignatius Press, 1987).

CHAPTER 3

Hope

In One Life

The man who came to be known as St. Augustine credited the grace of God and the persistence of one woman for leading him to faith. It was no easy task, but then nothing is impossible for God—and a determined mother.

A thumbnail sketch of Monica's life could be put into just a few phrases. Born around 331 in North Africa of Christian parents. Married Patricius, a pagan Roman official, at an early age. Three children: Augustine, Navigius, and Perpetua. Converted husband and mother-in-law in 370. Widowed in 371. Spent years praying for eldest child, who was brilliant but not concerned with morality. Followed him to Rome in 383 and then to Milan, where he joined the church on Easter Day in 387. Died later that year.

In his *Confessions*, which uses the style of speaking directly to God, Augustine explained that he skipped some details of his life because he was writing quickly. "But," he commented, "I will not pass over whatever my soul brings to birth concerning that handmaiden of yours [of God], who brought me to birth, both in her flesh, so that I was born into this temporal light, and in her heart, that I might be born to eternal light. Not of her gifts, but of your gifts in her, will I speak."

As young children, Monica and her sisters were under the care of an "age-worn maidservant" who had worked for the family for years. The maid was a strict tutor who "taught them with prudence and sobriety." This is pure speculation, but perhaps the maid recognized that some members of the family had a weakness for alcohol. She did not allow the children under her care to drink water except during meals, "even though they were parched with thirst." Her fear, Augustine said, was that when these women were in charge of households with wine cellars, "the habit of drinking will persist." Her goal then was to turn "the girls' thirst toward a virtuous moderation, so that even then they would not want to do what they should not do."

The maid's plan didn't work. A love of wine "crept on" Monica. "For when her parents, according to custom, ordered her . . . to fetch wine out of the cask, she would dip a cup into the opening at the top before she poured the wine into a pitcher." She'd take just a sip, Augustine wrote, because she didn't like the taste. Why did she do it? "Not out of a desire for drink, but from a sort of excess of those youthful spirits which blow off in absurd actions." It was a little naughty, a little daring, a little rebellious.

Still a young girl, Monica began to drink a bit more each time until, eventually, "she had fallen into the habit of greedily drinking her little cups almost full up with wine." She stopped, what we would call cold turkey, after she was in the cellar with a maid one day and the two of them got into an argument. Insults were exchanged, and the maid ended up calling Monica a lush, a "wine bibber" in the language of the day. "Wounded through and through by this taunt, she [Monica] beheld her own foul state, and immediately condemned it and cast it off," wrote Augustine.

When she "arrived at a marriageable age" —and at the time that could mean twelve— "she was given to her husband and served him 'as her lord.'" Monica "strove to win him to you [God], speaking to him about you through her conduct." She did this despite the fact Patricius was "given to violent anger" and slept around.

("She endured offenses against her marriage bed" is how one translation reads.)

At the same time, "by her good services and perseverance in patience and meekness, she also won over her mother-in-law," who, at first, hadn't cared for Monica at all (especially after hearing some of the lies "malicious servants" had been spreading about the younger woman). In contrast, Monica "showed herself to be a great peacemaker between persons who were at odds and in disagreement."

Patricius converted shortly before his death. His baptism—and that of her mother-in-law—came as a tremendous relief to Monica because, at that time, the common understanding was that anyone who had not been baptized (or died for the faith, which we would call baptism of blood) went to hell. It was that simple. That final. That was why Monica felt she could not rest until Augustine also joined the church and why she begged her son to become a Christian and wept bitterly when he continued to refuse. "Out of the blood of my mother's heart, through the tears she poured out by day and night, a sacrifice was offered up to you [God] in my behalf," Augustine wrote, "and you dealt with me in a wondrous way."

Born in 354, Augustine went away to school in Carthage in 370 to study rhetoric and look into becoming a lawyer. Instead he began to write. He also took a mistress with whom he had a son in 372. Augustine became interested in philosophy and then embraced a religious sect called Manichaeism. He taught for a decade and then decided to go to Rome.

Monica wanted to go with him, but he didn't want her there. So "I pretended that I had a friend whom I would not leave until a fair wind came and he could sail away," Augustine recalled. "Thus I lied to my mother—to such a mother!—and slipped away from her." Monica had refused to leave the area near the dock, but Augustine persuaded her to spend the night in a chapel not far away. Then he secretly set out, leaving her there "praying and weeping."

She still hoped that her child would be baptized. It seemed her prayer was not going to be answered when Augustine ditched her. But "in your deepest counsels you heard the crux of her desires," Augustine wrote. "You had no care for what she then sought, so that you might do for me what she forever sought."

God didn't grant her what she wanted then and there: to go to Rome with Augustine. He would give her what she truly desired: Augustine joining the church. In the meantime, her faith didn't falter. She kept her end of the agreement. She continued to pray for Augustine and continued to lead an exemplary life as "a chaste and sober . . . widow, generous in almsgiving, faithful and helpful to your holy ones, letting no day pass without offering at your altar, going without fail to church twice a day, in the morning and evening . . . that she might hear you in your instructions and that you might hear her in her prayers."

Later Monica also traveled to Rome. When Augustine told her that he had abandoned his Manichaean philosophy but had not yet accepted Christianity, he expected her to be very pleased. She wasn't. "Rather," he recalled, "she was all the more certain that you [God], who had promised the whole, would grant what still remained."

Years before, in a dream, Monica had seen Augustine with her, "where she was." She understood this to mean in the church. She never lost sight of that. She never lost hope. "By this dream of joy of that holy woman, to be fulfilled so long afterwards, was predicted much beforehand so as to bring consolation in her then present solicitude."

It was what kept her going when her request seemed impossible.

Even as she wept and worried and even plotted a bit, she never doubted that God would give her what she asked. A year later, when Augustine accepted a teaching position in Milan, she asked for help from the bishop there, St. Ambrose. At Monica's urging, Augustine became engaged, but the girl was still too young to get married (she was probably about ten). Then his common-law wife left him and their son, Adeodatus.

Monica, of course, was hoping marriage would encourage Augustine to settle down and join the church. No stranger to deep and wondrous prayer, she asked God for a vision to show that this, too, was God's plan. It never came.

Instead, Augustine turned to Christ with an open and contrite heart. And God "turned her mourning into a joy far richer than that she had desired, far deeper and purer than that she had sought in grandchildren born of my flesh."

Augustine would go on to become a priest and then a bishop. In time, he became one of the greatest teachers in the church and one of its most ardent defenders. His mother didn't live to see this. Soon after Augustine's baptism, Monica "fell sick of fever." Augustine and his entourage, including his son, had been preparing to sail back to North Africa.

Monica knew she was at the end of her life on earth. A great concern of hers had always been that she be buried back in North Africa beside her husband, Patricius. But when her final days arrived, she told Augustine and his brother, Navigius, "Put this body away anywhere. Don't let care about it disturb you. I ask only this of you, that you remember me at the altar of the Lord, wherever you may be."

The death of his mother devastated Augustine, even as the faith and hope that had guided her life became his own. He came to trust in God's mercy. "Because you are not rigorous in searching out sins," he wrote, "we confidently hope to find a place with you."

Two years later, his son died.

Later in life, when Augustine wrote of these things, he asked that those who read his story say a prayer for both his parents and not forget this woman of faith and hope and love. "Inspire, O my Lord, my God, inspire your servants my brethren, your sons my masters, whom with voice and heart and pen I serve, so that as many of them as read these words may at your altar remember Monica, your handmaid . . . so that, more abundantly than through my own prayers, my mother's last request of me may be granted through the prayers of many."

We, too, remember Monica in prayer—not by praying to God for her as Augustine did, but by praying to her to intercede for us, that the hope that guided her life might also direct our own.

In Scripture

The Hebrew of the Old Testament doesn't have just one single word that's a perfect match for our English word *hope*. We know what we mean when we say hope: to desire something, often with the expectation that our desire will be fulfilled.

In the Old Testament, the two words used most frequently to give the idea of hope are *kawah*, which means "to wait for," and, as we discussed in the previous chapter, *batah*, "to trust or have confidence." But those aren't the only ones. English translations also use *hope* for other Hebrew words that mean "to seek refuge" or "to expect."

For whom did the chosen people wait? In whom did the individual Israelite place his or her trust? Yahweh, the "hope of Israel" (Jeremiah 14:8); the Lord, "my hope" (Psalm 71:5).

On the other hand, the person who placed hope in a human being didn't stand a chance. How did the Israelites know this? God told them. "Thus says the Lord: Cursed are those who trust in mere mortals" (Jeremiah 17:5). No, the nation and each of its people were not to look to their own justice or strength. Not to neighboring Egypt, to princes, to pride, or to lying words. Not to riches. Their refuge, their fortress, was God alone.

Just as the Old Testament is the story of faith—the people find it, lose it, reclaim it, abuse it, toss it, cling to it, and, through it all, manage to keep that flame alive—it is also the story of hope. In the Pentateuch, the patriarchs

Abraham, Isaac, Jacob, and the others hope that their descendants will become the great people God has promised they will become. Those descendants hope for the land the Lord has said will be theirs.

In a certain sense, after the kingdom of Israel falls to the Assyrians at the end of the eighth century B.C. and the kingdom of Judah (southern Israel) falls to the Babylonians at the beginning of the sixth, the stakes grow higher. Do they dare to hope now? There was no one to rescue them but Yahweh. He alone could provide "a door of hope" (Hosea 2:15).

Many of the prophets preached of the need to quietly wait for God, and over time, that idea evolved into the confident belief that the Lord would deliver his people not simply from their present troubles but from all troubles, from all sorrow, from all pain.

In this wondrous new order, "the wolf shall live with the lamb, the leopard shall lie down with the kid, the calf and the lion and the fatling together, and a little child shall lead them. The cow and the bear shall graze, their young shall lie down together; and the lion shall eat straw like the ox. The nursing child shall play over the hole of the asp, and the weaned child shall put its hand on the adder's den. They will not hurt or destroy on all my holy mountain; for the earth will be full of the knowledge of the Lord as the waters cover the sea" (Isaiah 11:6–9).

But, at the same time, through almost the entire Old Testament, any sense of hope ends abruptly and completely with death. Except for the very last parts of this collection of books, there's no idea of life going beyond the grave.

One may hope for the lives of one's descendants, but hope for oneself ends with death. So Job, having lost his children, his health, and his property, laments, "My days are swifter than a weaver's shuttle, and come to their end without hope" (Job 7:6). Though there may be "hope for a tree, if it is cut down, that it will sprout again, and that its shoots will not cease" (14:7), death is the end of human hope because "mortals die, and are laid low; humans expire, and where are they?" (14:10).

No, to be dead is to be without hope. When the people of Israel are in exile, their condition is compared to that of a man who has perished. "Mortal, these bones are the whole house of Israel. They say, 'Our bones are dried up, and our hope is lost'" (Ezekiel 37:11).

Only in the later books of the Old Testament is there a glimmer of hope that God's love and power will find a way to show themselves beyond the grave. A hint is given when Job proclaims, "For I know that my Redeemer lives, and . . . in my flesh I shall see God" (Job

19:25–26). More explicitly, Wisdom affirms, "The souls of the righteous are in the hand of God, and no torment will ever touch them. In the eyes of the foolish they seemed to have died, and their departure was thought to be a disaster, and their going from us to be their destruction; but they are at peace" (Wisdom 3:1–3).

It is as if these faint hints of hope in the later Old Testament are building toward the full and startling revelation of hope that is given in the New Testament: Jesus has risen from the dead, and all those who believe in him will one day do the same.

Elpis and *elpizein* are the Greek words for hope that can be found in the New Testament. Meaning "expectation" or "to expect," in secular Greek they were "neutral" in that they could refer to an expected good or an expected evil. In the New Testament, these words are always directed toward something good.

In the writings of Paul, especially in Romans, the theological concept of hope is most fully examined and explained. Paul uses Abraham as the model for hope, which shouldn't be surprising. If the patriarch is the model for true faith, then how can he help but be an example of true hope? "Hoping against hope," Paul says of him, "he believed that he would become 'the father of many nations'" (Romans 4:18). Some Scripture scholars say that passage would be better translated to read "hoping against expectation."

What Abraham hoped for was beyond what any reasonable person would expect, but then faith drives home the message that, with God, anything is possible. "For in hope we were saved," Paul writes a few verses later and instructs that "hope that is seen is not hope. For who hopes for what is seen? But if we hope for what we do not see, we wait for it with patience" (Romans 8:24–25).

What is it the Christian cannot see but for which he or she hopes? In a word, the *doxa*, or glory of God and Christ. We have cut ourselves off from that glory by sin (Romans 3:23), but "since we are justified by faith, we have peace with God through our Lord Jesus Christ, through whom we have obtained access to this grace in which we stand; and we boast in our hope of sharing the glory of God" (Romans 5:1–2).

Because of Christ, Paul writes, we hope in salvation, life everlasting, the kingdom of God. We hope in "what no eye has seen, nor ear heard, nor the human heart conceived, what God has prepared for those who love him" (1 Corinthians 2:9, referring back to Isaiah 64:4).

Paul is saying Christian hope is eschatological. That means it looks to the end of time. It looks beyond time. It firmly trusts in what no human can see, what no human can know. It trusts God. It trusts Christ. It believes what God has promised and what Christ has done. Faith gives us reason to hope.

To be a Christian, then, is to be a person of hope. In contrast, Paul reminds the Ephesians, "remember that you were at that time without Christ, being aliens from the commonwealth of Israel, and strangers to the covenants of promise, having no hope and without God in the world" (2:12).

But, Paul makes clear, being with God in the world doesn't mean those who follow Jesus are spared pain and suffering. It isn't yet Isaiah's hoped-for new order (the lion and the lamb getting along just fine) where troubles simply don't exist. Not by a long shot. In a sense, just the opposite is true. "We also boast in our sufferings," the apostle writes, "knowing that suffering produces endurance, and endurance produces character, and character produces hope" (Romans 5:3–4). This means a Christian does not face suffering with the same attitude and resignation as a tough-it-out Stoic. In that form of philosophy, which was popular at the time, there was no hope (although its classical virtues were wisdom, courage, justice, and temperance). Instead, the ones who follow Christ "suffer with him so that we may also be glorified with him" (Romans 8:17).

Hard times will always be a part of life, but "by steadfastness and by the encouragement of the scriptures we might have hope" (Romans 15:4). Hope doesn't take away pain; it gives it purpose. And that hope, Paul writes, "does not disappoint us, because God's love has been poured into our hearts through the Holy Spirit that has been given to us" (Romans 5:5).

Down through the Ages

If we want to know about hope, St. Augustine wrote, we have only to say the Our Father. That's because the many things Jesus and the church have taught about this virtue "are contained in the Lord's Prayer."

St. Augustine, the bishop of Hippo in northern Africa, is best known for the *Confessions* and the *City of God*. In *On Faith, Hope and Charity*, he explained how the prayer Jesus taught his disciples is the very essence of hope.

Augustine began by reminding his readers that "Divine Scriptures testify" that "cursed be every man that putteth hope in man." (A more modern translation of Jeremiah 17:5 is "Cursed are those who trust in mere mortals.") That means, the bishop wrote, "he who puts hope in himself is also ensnared in the chain of this curse."

"Therefore," Augustine continued, "we ought to make petition only from the Lord God, whatever it be that we hope to do well or to obtain as a reward for good works." In Matthew's Gospel (6:9–13), Augustine said, "the Lord's Prayer is seen to contain seven petitions, in three of which eternal goods are asked for, in the remaining four, temporal goods; yet these are necessary for obtaining the eternal goods."

By saying "Hallowed be thy name," "thy kingdom come," and "thy will be done on earth, as it is in heaven," we "ask for blessings that are to be retained forever." They start "in this life," Augustine said, and "are increased in us as we progress." As we grow in grace, these blessings do the same. That continues until we die and reach heaven. Then "in their perfection, which is to be looked for in another life, they will be owned forevermore."

When we say "Give us this day our daily bread. And forgive us our debts, as we also forgive our debtors. And lead us not into temptation, but deliver us from evil," who, asked Augustine, "does not see that this pertains to the needs of the present life?" These petitions, these things we hope for, center on us here and now, still on earth.

When we get to heaven, to that "eternal life, where we all hope to be," said Augustine, "the making hallowed of his name, his kingdom, and his will in our spirit and body, will be perfected and will abide everlastingly. But daily bread is so called because it is necessary in this life, in whatever amount the soul or the body demands, whether we interpret the word in reference to the spirit, or the flesh, or in both senses."

As creatures made up of body and soul, we need "daily bread"—food, shelter, clothing, health, employment, and so on—to mature, thrive physically, and grow spiritually. In the same way, we ask for, and hope for, forgiveness for the sins we have committed. We ask that we be able to avoid temptations, that we don't sin. That we be saved from evil, from the horrifying consequences of sins, both our own and others. "But none of those is to be found in the other life," St. Augustine noted. In heaven, we don't need "daily bread." Our sins have been forgiven, and we will not sin again. And because there is no sin, the consequences of sin are not there.

Everything good we can hope for is in the Our Father. Everything we need here and now. Everything we will enjoy with God forever in heaven. When the disciples asked Jesus point-blank how to pray, he gave them, and us, this prayer. This is what you are to ask for, Christ was saying. This is what you are to want. This is what you are to hope for.

In the sixteenth century, the Spanish mystic St. John of the Cross associated faith with the intellect, hope with the memory, and charity with the will. That can seem odd to us since we think of memory as having to do with the past and hope with the future, but in St. John's understanding of the human psyche, the memory is a kind of habitual self-awareness, like consciousness. So faith has to do with what we know (but goes beyond rational knowing), hope has to do with our personal self-awareness, and charity has to do with commitment of the will, what we do.

St. John taught in *The Ascent of Mount Carmel* that through contemplation a person could go beyond intellect, memory, and will to attain faith, hope, and love. "In order to journey to God," St. John said, "the intellect must be perfected in the darkness of faith, the memory in the emptiness of hope, and the will in the nakedness and absence of every affection."

Faith involves not intellectual light but a kind of darkness: we don't see what we believe in. Hope involves an emptiness, a self-forgetfulness. And love implies a nakedness of the will and an absence of affection.

That sounds pretty bleak, but for St. John of the Cross, that's where we start: with a recognition of our own emptiness. Then we discover the fullness of God that exceeds all our expectations. Through faith, hope, and charity, we are united to God in this life. So we can't try to "do it ourselves" by our own smug brilliance (intellect), sense of self-importance (memory), or attachment to things that are less than God (will, or the love of creature rather than Creator).

With regard to hope, the mystic explained that "hope always pertains to the unpossessed object. If something were possessed there could no longer be hope for it." That makes sense. If a child hopes to get a bicycle for Christmas, that hope vanishes Christmas morning when she spots a two-wheeler with her name on it standing next to the tree in the living room. Once a hope is fulfilled, it's gone.

That's why, St. John said, "this virtue also occasions emptiness, since it is concerned with unpossessed things and not with the possessed object." Hope isn't about what we have, it's about what we *don't* have. By entering the "dark night" (being led by faith, hope, and love rather than by our own "lights"), we overcome the power of self-love and so "journey by as straight and short a road" as we can.

In the latter half of the twentieth century, German philosopher Josef Pieper used the image of a journey to describe the nature of hope.

Pieper, who died in 1997, noted in *On Hope* that the idea that each human is "a pilgrim on this earth" is "part of the very foundation of being in the world for the Christian: the concept of the *status viatoris* is one of the basic concepts of every Christian rule of life."

To be a *viator* means to be "one on the way," he explained, translating the Latin. So the *status viatoris* is "the condition or state of being on the way." Its opposite is *status comprehensoris;* that's one who has comprehended or arrived. The *viator* is making progress toward eternal happiness. The *comprehensor* has reached that ultimate goal.

Pieper was careful to point out that "the state of being on the way is not to be understood in a primary and literal sense as a designation of place." Rather, it refers "to the innermost structure of created nature. It is the inherent 'not yet' of the finite being." (A cake is not a cake until it is baked. An "unbaked cake" is cake batter.)

When we sin, we, in Pieper's words, turn toward "nothingness" rather than completion. We came from nothingness, "from dust" as an Ash Wednesday blessing reminds us, yet we were created to be with God, to "arrive." On earth, we are between those extremes, and because of free will (a God-given gift), we have the power to choose which way we move.

For the person who realizes "the not-yet-existing-being" of his own existence, "there is only one appropriate answer to such an experience," Pieper said. "This answer must be despair—for the meaning of the creature's existence is not nothingness but being, that is, fulfillment."

"The only answer that corresponds to man's actual existential situation is hope," he wrote. "The virtue of hope is preeminently the virtue of the *status viatoris;* it is the proper virtue of the 'not yet.'"

In the virtue of hope more than any other virtue, Pieper maintained, "man understands and affirms that he is a creature, that he has been created by God." As a theological virtue, it is "an ennobling of man's nature that entirely surpasses what he 'can be' of himself."

Commercials for the United States Army urge potential recruits to "be all that you can be." But the theological virtues are the way each of us can be, not "all that we can be," but *more* than we can be. And "this supernatural potentiality for being is grounded in a real, grace-filled participation in the divine nature, which comes to man through Christ," Pieper wrote.

Following Jesus, being a person of hope, makes us more than we can be. "Hope," Pieper said, "expects from God's hand the eternal life that is God himself." And "prayer and hope are naturally ordered to each other. Prayer is the expression and proclamation of hope. . . . Hope itself speaks through it."

When the disciples asked to be taught how to pray, Christ knew they were asking him how to hope.

Of course. "Hope . . . cannot exist," Pieper concluded, "except from, through and in Christ."

For Us Today

Hope can seem like the little virtue in the middle—the one that gets aced out of the way, shouldered aside by faith and love.

Who ever prays "Lord, give me hope"? Should we even bother? Certainly.

We need this scrappy virtue, this little one that doesn't give in and doesn't give up. We can hope even as our faith is rocked by doubt. We can hope even as we feel unloved and unlovable. It isn't that faith no longer exists, that love is only a thing of the past; it's simply that at times we fail to recognize them. At that moment—that dark, frightening, middle-of-the-night period in our lives—a tiny spark of hope shines brightly. It warms us. It reassures us.

But we need the virtue of hope in the light of day, too. We need that image and vision that show us what our life on earth can be like.

We can make the mistake of assuming that hope, or any of the other virtues, can be tied down to "religion" alone as we box in "religion" to mean only what happens in a church building. Only what happens at Mass. Only what happens when we formally pray.

But hope, like all the other virtues, is meant to be a part of our entire life, part of all that we experience. This is a virtue we can call on and rely on, not just to help guide us toward God's kingdom in heaven, but to allow us to better understand how that kingdom has already begun on earth. It can help us realize all the good things, all the graces, we need during our time on earth. It can help us ask for and work toward our "daily bread" of all those blessings that we crave, body and soul.

Take the example of a young engaged couple. Naturally, they hope for a happy marriage. They can see themselves in their own home. They can see the life they will live together. They can see the product, the blossoming, the fruit of the love they share—their children. They can see themselves growing older. They can see happiness and joy and contentment and companionship stretching ahead for decades.

Or consider a college or graduate student. She can see herself in the profession for which she is aiming. There she is, now a teacher, standing in front of the classroom. There she is, now a doctor, stepping into the examination room to greet a patient. There she is designing a computer program, putting the finishing touches on her business plan, playing the opening notes of a concerto to a standing-room-only audience.

More than simple imagination, hope is what gives us the ability to move from "that could be done" to "that could be done by me." Psychologists who work with athletes say this is a key to personal achievement. The baseball player who is in a hitting slump sees himself at the plate swinging, connecting, heading for first base. He replays that image over and over again. The golfer does it with her drive. The quarterback with his pass.

Motivational speakers preach that this is what makes success in the business world possible. They each offer variations on the maxim "If my mind can conceive it and my heart can believe it, I know I can achieve it."

That's a part of hope. But that's not all it is.

Sometimes no matter how much we hope for something, no matter how much we work toward it, we don't get what we wanted. It could be that our desires change. It could be that our dreams go unfulfilled. The student teacher could realize she doesn't like being in front of the classroom. It isn't as she imagined it would be. Or it could be she has to drop out of college because of a financial crunch. She can't afford to get her degree and her teaching certificate.

Where is hope then? Has it let her down? Has it deceived her? Hope may have disappeared with the realization that what she had hoped for she no longer wants. (Few adults still hope they'll get a Barbie or BB gun for Christmas.) But maybe what she hoped for, what she still hopes for, she now has to accept will never be. (The young athlete dreams of a professional career, and then a serious injury makes that impossible.) When life—for whatever reason and in whatever manner—tears hope from our heart, there can be tremendous pain and sorrow.

And that will happen. There is no avoiding it because we live in an imperfect world. We live in a world where sin can lead to tragedy but also a world where sometimes, as with Job, bad things happen to good people.

We hoped for a long and happy marriage, but it fell apart through selfishness or neglect. It fell apart because a partner was no longer willing to make it work. Because getting married to this person in the first place was a mistake.

We hoped for a long and happy marriage, but it ended when a drunk driver killed our partner. When cancer or heart disease or ALS stole him or her from us. Maybe there is someone to blame, and maybe there isn't. Either way, grief has replaced hope.

Always, always, in every human being's life, there is suffering. There is what appears to be the end of any reason to hope. There is understandable cause for despair.

• • •

It's important that we make a distinction here between that kind of despair and true clinical depression. It's like the difference between having a "broken heart" and having a heart attack. Clinical depression, like a heart attack, is a physical ailment that needs to be treated.

Depression is more than feeling down, more than "the blues." Overcoming it is not simply a matter of thinking happy thoughts, a matter of becoming a person of hope, a matter of toughing it out. To use another analogy, appendicitis cannot be remedied by happy thoughts, by hoping, or by toughing it out. Depression is an illness that needs medical attention, usually a combination of medication and therapy.

We mention all this here because clinical depression smothers hope and with it, sadly and too often, the desire to go on living. Without hope of any kind, the world's pains appear too great, too merciless. Life here becomes a true hell, a place, or rather a condition, in which there is no hope.

It would be misguided to look to the virtue of hope to "treat" clinical depression just as it would be to think increasing the virtue of love in our life could take the place of needed heart surgery. It would be incorrect to assume clinical depression is somehow a "sin" against the virtue of hope just as it would be to think a clogging of the heart's arteries is a "sin" against the virtue of love.

• • •

We know we hope. We know sometimes what we hope for doesn't come to be. We know we hurt because of that. What, then, can St. Paul's words mean for us today? "We also boast in our sufferings, knowing that suffering produces endurance, and endurance produces character, and character produces hope."

Is it possible the dashed hopes that cause our suffering can be the signs that lead to hope? Perhaps suffering helps us refine our hopes and sharpen our focus on what we hope for. Perhaps it helps lead us to realize there is one thing for which we can hope and toward which we can work that is beyond and above all other hopes.

Our "daily bread" hopes, good though they might be, are for here and now. At best, when fulfilled, they guide us toward the ultimate hope: life with God.

But even when we understand this as much as we're able to, suffering does not lose its sting. The death of a dream or a loved one still causes us to grieve even as it forces us to consider what comes after that death.

Our faith and the hope that springs from that faith say life will win in the end. Against what we can see and hear and feel, against what we can explain and measure and prove, there is eternal life. There is the hope of being with our loved one again, of sharing paradise with him or her forever.

How, here and now, do we increase the virtue of hope within us? We actively look for and recognize reasons to hope. We examine what we are hoping for. Is it part of God's will, or do we hope for things that will turn us, to use Josef Pieper's word, toward "nothingness"? And we accept the fact that disappointments and broken dreams don't mean there's no reason to hope. They may, in fact, be the stepping stones to more authentic, more profound, more grace-filled hope.

A person of hope is not some Pollyanna, refusing to see what is obvious. Rather, a person of hope is one who trusts in what can only be seen through faith and reached through love.

"Hope," the *Catechism of the Catholic Church* reminds us, "is the theological virtue by which we desire the kingdom of heaven and eternal life as our happiness, placing our trust in Christ's promises and relying not on our own strength, but on the help of the grace of the Holy Spirit."

God gives us this hope as he gives us himself. He is our hope.

To Read More about It

Augustine, *The Confessions,* trans. Maria Boulding, O.S.B. (Hyde Park, N.Y.: New City Press, 1997).

Bernard Haring, *Hope Is the Remedy* (New York: Doubleday, 1972).

John of the Cross, *The Collected Works of St. John of the Cross,* trans. Kieran Kavanaugh, O.C.D., and Otilio Rodriguez, O.C.D. (Washington, D.C.: ICS Publications, 1973).

Josef Pieper, *On Hope* (San Francisco: Ignatius Press, 1986).

CHAPTER 4

Love

In One Life

When Pope John XXIII canonized Martin de Porres on May 6, 1962, he said this about the Dominican brother: "He excused the faults of others. He forgave the bitterest injuries, convinced that he deserved much severer punishments on account of his own sins. He tried with all his might to redeem the guilty; lovingly he comforted the sick; he provided food, shelter and medicine for the poor; he helped, as best he could, farm laborers and Negroes, as well as mulattoes, who were looked upon at the time as akin to slaves; thus he deserved to be called by the name the people gave him: 'Martin of Charity.'"

Martin de Porres was familiar with poverty. He knew racism. He understood what it felt like to be a child abandoned by a parent.

He had reasons, good reasons, to be bitter, angry, and self-centered, but instead he chose to be the opposite. He chose love.

The baptismal record for the infant boy born in Lima, Peru, on November 9, 1579, read "father unknown." It was a lie. He was the illegitimate child of Anna Velasquez and Juan de Porres. Velasquez was a freed black woman, the daughter of Panamanian slaves. De Porres was a Spanish knight and the future governor of Panama.

Martin and his sister, Juana, also the child of de Porres and Velasquez, had features that favored their mother. The derogatory term for their appearance was "half-breed" or "war souvenir." The acceptable one was "mulatto." No matter what word was used, their looks were why their father would have nothing to do with them.

Anna Velasquez raised her children in poverty until Martin was eight. At that point, the boy's kindness and openness won over his father. At the age of twelve, young Martin was apprenticed to a barber-surgeon who taught him not only how to cut hair but also how to draw blood (then considered the proper remedy for many ailments), take care of wounds, and administer medication.

Both as a child and as an adolescent, Martin was known for his love of prayer. In time, this blossomed into a religious vocation. In 1594, he joined the Order of Preachers, the Dominicans, as a *donatus*, a lay helper or tertiary. Martin didn't feel he was worthy of becoming a brother and certainly not of being ordained a priest. Truth be told, society and some members of the order felt much the same way: the brotherhood or priesthood was no place for a mulatto.

The *donati* performed the most menial and physically taxing chores for the religious community, which was called a convent. Because Martin did the chores with such vigor, care, and love for nine years and because he demonstrated that same commitment in his personal piety, his fellow Dominicans came to him and asked him to become a fully professed brother. He accepted that invitation but declined ordination.

The people of the city of Lima, representing all classes and races, also came to know Brother Martin. They came to respect him, to depend on him, and to love him.

Until his death in 1639, Martin's life was like a candle. The wick was prayer; the wax was service. Dependent on each other, they shared a common flame: love. Martin spent long hours in prayer, not just with fellow community members as part of the daily schedule, but alone in the chapel and in his room at night. His housemates couldn't help but notice that strange things happened when the young brother prayed. At times, he was in ecstasy, unaware of the world around him. At times light filled the room. At times he was seen elevated, floating in the air. It's said the men with whom he lived became so accustomed to these phenomena that a priest once casually mentioned to a guest, "You'll soon get used to Brother Martin's heavenly favors."

Of course, during his early years in the convent, there were others who assumed the young Dominican was a fake. They suspected he was performing tricks to draw attention to himself. But his actions, including miracles that helped others, proved that wasn't the case. Sometimes he cured people, not with his knowledge and skill in medicine, but with a saintly touch. When that happened, he would be embarrassed and try to explain away the miracle, but the people knew what they saw. They knew it wasn't medicine but Martin. And they flocked to him.

There were other extraordinary sights. People said he had the ability to bilocate (to be in two places at the same time), including being in another country on another continent. Word spread that he covered distances at the speed of light, earning him the nickname "the Flying Brother."

Martin rose each morning at four to greet the dawn in honor of Mary. It's said she frequently appeared to him, holding the child Jesus in her arms. She spoke with Martin and helped him when he was taking care of the sick and the poor.

There was another aspect of Brother Martin's spirituality, one that was commonly accepted at the time but has since fallen out of favor. This aspect was personal mortification that went beyond denying oneself simple pleasures such as giving up sweets, fasting, and such. Martin would "take the discipline," which meant scourging himself, three times a day. Partly symbolic, there was also pain involved in the practice.

At the same time all these things were happening, Martin was working both inside and outside the convent. Inside, his duties included kitchen work, laundry, and cleaning. In the evening, he would visit the servants' quarters to treat any of their ailments, and he frequently took care of the community's horses. His love for animals became legendary. Often St. Martin is depicted with a mouse at his feet. It's said that when traps were set in the convent, Martin asked that another method be tried first. He told the mice to leave the building and stay outside. He promised to feed them in the garden each day if they did. They obeyed him. (He also kept stray cats and dogs at his sister's house.)

His duties outside the community included taking care of anyone who showed up at the convent's infirmary needing medical help. In effect, he ran a modern drop-in clinic, one that practiced no discrimination. He was also placed in charge of distributing food to the poor.

Martin had the ability to raise money to fund the clinic, the "food bank," and other projects. His sources were not heavenly but, considering the donors, were in a sense miraculous. At that time, less than a century after the conquest of Peru, the country had its fair share of conquerors and fortune hunters, those who had acquired great wealth by, at best, questionable means. At that point in their lives, some wanted to do good and help others. (It seems safe to speculate that a sizable portion of them were in the latter stages of this life and seriously wondering about the next.) It was said they gave Martin the equivalent of thousands of dollars each week.

They trusted him. They knew any money given to him wouldn't end up in his or someone else's pocket. They saw what he was doing.

After coming upon so many abandoned children on Lima's mean streets, Martin began a hostel and a school for the youngsters. In time, with the approval of the viceroy and the archbishop and with a hefty donation from a local businessman, this came to be the Orphanage of the Holy Cross.

The Dominican brother was also known and welcomed at a seaport some five miles away where soldiers were stationed at a military post. They had only the bare essentials. Martin brought them food and clothing. Some of the money he collected was used to provide dowries for young women who otherwise couldn't afford to get married or enter religious life. Other funds went to the care of slaves who had been brought to Peru from Africa.

Year after year throughout his life, just as light filled the room in which he prayed by himself at night, love filled the city in which he worked with, and for, others during the day.

When Martin died at the age of sixty, thousands from all walks of life attended his funeral. They came to mourn this unassuming man who loved so deeply yet all the while considered himself—in his own words—"only a poor mulatto."

In Scripture

What did *love* mean in Scripture? Many things, from religious adoration to sweaty romance.

The Old Testament words that come from the root *'āhab* have many meanings. God's love for human beings. Humans' love for God. The love shared between people who are a part of a religious community.

But the words can also mean the love a parent has for a child (Genesis 22:2), the love spouses share (Genesis 24:67), friendship (1 Samuel 18:1, 3), the dependence a slave has on the kindness of his or her master (Exodus 21:5), and even sexual passion (2 Samuel 13:1, 4).

When the Old Testament Hebrew was later translated into Greek, three words were used for the *'āhab* words. Forms of *eros* and *philia* appear infrequently. Variations on *agape* are by far the most common. (That's the word found so often in the New Testament, and it takes on particular meaning there.) Scripture scholars point out that the use of *agape* words in the Old Testament doesn't always fill the bill. These words lack the emotion, the fire, of the *'āhab* words.

When *agape* was translated from Greek to Latin, it became *caritas* rather than *amor. Amor* was considered a little too naughty. In English, *caritas* is *charity* in some translations and *love* in others. Some scholars prefer *charity* because at its root is the same word that gives us the French word *cher* and, with it, the idea of holding something close to the heart and cherishing it.

The Old Testament is the story of a people finding out there is a God who loves—even cherishes—them, and they are to do the same in return. The story of creation is God's love in action. He makes humans in his own image and richly blesses them. Even when they turn from him, he doesn't abandon them but promises he will save them in the future (Genesis 3:14).

As time goes by and Yahweh reveals himself more and more to his chosen people, they discover he is "merciful and gracious, slow to anger, and abounding in steadfast love and faithfulness, keeping steadfast love for the thousandth generation, forgiving iniquity and transgression and sin." In fact, those are the Lord's words to Moses, describing himself (Exodus 34:6–7).

The people find out God expects them to serve him, to keep his commandments, and to love him in return. Even more, he requires it. His message to Moses continues with the warning "Yet by no means clearing the guilty, but visiting the iniquity of the parents upon the children and the children's children, to the third and the fourth generation."

The Israelites also discover that, fortunately, God's justice is always tempered with merciful kindness. "I have loved you with an everlasting love," he tells them, "therefore I have continued my faithfulness to you" (Jeremiah 31:3). His "steadfast love endures forever" (Jeremiah 33:11) even when, like a spouse who cheats on his or her partner, the chosen people turn to false gods. Then, like that injured

spouse who wants the marriage to endure, their
Creator tries to win them back (Jeremiah 3).
The covenant they share, like marriage, is a
bond of love.

It isn't just the nation of Israel that can
enter into this bond but its individual members
as well. God loves each of them. They submit
themselves to him and place themselves in his
care, and so they are his children, his friends
(Wisdom 5:5; 7:27). They, as individuals and as
a people, show their love for God by obeying
his commandments, but they must do that not
legalistically but passionately. With all their
"heart and soul" (Deuteronomy 4:29). With
thankfulness and trust (Deuteronomy 8:1–20).

"Those who trust in him will understand
truth, and the faithful will abide with him in
love, because grace and mercy are upon his
holy ones, and he watches over his elect" (Wisdom 3:9). In fact, to love wisdom is to love
God, while "those who despise wisdom and
instruction are miserable" (Wisdom 3:11).
Conversely, "the fear of the Lord"—loving
God wholeheartedly—"is the beginning of wisdom" (Psalm 111:10). Why is this so? Because
God is truth. God is wisdom.

In late Judaism, three times a day the
Hebrews were to stop and recall that all-
encompassing relationship as they prayed:
"You shall love the Lord your God with all

your heart, and with all your soul, and with all your might" (Deuteronomy 6:5). This, Jesus said, was the greatest commandment (Matthew 22:36–38). But what about the one he said was the second greatest? "You shall love your neighbor as yourself."

That, too, can be found in the Old Testament. Jesus is quoting Leviticus 19:18. To the chosen people, that would first mean loving fellow Israelites, but it was broadened to include foreigners and even enemies, who are to be forgiven rather than hated. What's unique in Jesus' teaching is that he brings the two laws together, and he drives home concretely what it means to be a neighbor in the parable of the Good Samaritan (Luke 10:29–37).

But in the New Testament, the most central and important meaning of *agape* is the love God has for humanity. He is "the God of love" (2 Corinthians 13:11). His love is that of a father, and it extends even to sinners. He is the Good Shepherd (Luke 15:4–7), the father who rushes out to welcome back the prodigal (Luke 15:11–32).

And this heavenly Father's love is revealed and given to us through Christ, his "beloved." God so loved the world that he sent his Son to atone for humanity's sins. Salvation in Christ is the highest, the ultimate, proof of God's love.

To love the Son is to love the Father. That love, on our part, includes obedience; it is following God's commandments. But it is also self-denial. It is carrying our own cross. The love we show God is really only a share of the love that proceeds from God. In other words, God fills our hearts with love—he pours love into our hearts by the Holy Spirit—and we return it to him.

Our human love is always simply that. It is not something we achieve. It is not a virtue we attain by our own powers or efforts. It is, borrowing the term later used in theology, a "divine" or "infused" virtue. We are able to love God because of God's grace. That love compels us to love our "neighbor." God's love calls us to serve others. God loves everyone. We are to imitate him. At the same time, all those who follow Christ are to share that *agape* with one another in a special way. This love shared in Christ has an eschatological dimension. It looks to the end of the world when he will come again.

Paul is careful to point out that this love also includes freedom. "For you were called to freedom, brothers and sisters; only do not use your freedom as an opportunity for self-indulgence, but through love become slaves to one another" (Galatians 5:13). This personal choice is essential to *agape*. God does not force us to love. But if we choose to love, then we cannot pick and choose whom we love.

In the thirteenth chapter of his first letter to the Corinthians, Paul offers what has become one of the best-known descriptions of this love (and of the uselessness of a life or any so-called achievement that doesn't include it). "If I speak in tongues of mortals and of angels, but do not have love, I am a noisy gong or a clanging cymbal. . . . Love is patient; love is kind; love is not envious or boastful or arrogant or rude. . . . Love never ends." John uses three words to sum up all revelation: "God is love" (1 John 4:8).

One final point: Any examination of the virtue of love has to include its relationship to the two other "divine" virtues—faith and hope.

Love is often associated with faith. "Keep alert, stand firm in your faith, be courageous, be strong. Let all that you do be done in love" (1 Corinthians 16:13). "Peace to the whole community, and love with faith, from God the Father and the Lord Jesus Christ" (Ephesians 6:23). "But Timothy has just now come to us from you, and has brought us the good news of your faith and love" (1 Thessalonians 3:6).

And frequently both are tied to hope. "We always give thanks to God for all of you and mention you in our prayers, constantly remembering before our God and Father your work of faith and labor of love and steadfastness of hope in our Lord Jesus Christ" (1 Thessalonians 1:2–3). "But since we belong to the day, let us be sober, and put on the breastplate of faith and love, and for a helmet the hope of salvation" (1 Thessalonians 5:8). "We have heard of your faith in Christ Jesus and of the love that you have for all the saints because of the hope laid up for you in heaven" (Colossians 1:4–5).

But, as Paul points out, love tops the other two. "And now faith, hope, and love abide, these three; and the greatest of these is love" (1 Corinthians 13:13). It is the ultimate virtue. In it are contained all others.

Down through the Ages

The top-ten list has been a regular feature on a late-night television show. A seventh-century Greek theologian penned several collections that might be called "Top 100s." And the category for each was love.

Using a style that was popular at the time, St. Maximus the Confessor (ca. 580–662) wrote "The Four Centuries on Charity" to help Christians better understand and live Jesus' message. Scholars say he chose the number four because there are four Gospels, and they contain the great commandment to love and the great example of God's love. Each "century" featured one hundred short sayings—maxims! —or instructions:

"He that loves God most certainly also loves his neighbor."

"He that flees from worldly desires places himself above every worldly grief."

"As a sparrow that is tied by the foot tries to fly but is dragged to the earth by the cord that holds it, so the mind that does not yet possess detachment, when it flies to knowledge of heavenly things, is drawn down by its passion and dragged to earth."

The truths and lessons St. Maximus was teaching can seem especially poignant to us because we know how his story ended. St. Maximus devoted much of his life to fighting a heresy called Monothelitism. It said Christ had two natures, human and divine, but only one will. The church teaches Jesus had both two natures and two wills. Far from being a dry, academic, and civilized debate, it was a fiery controversy that sparked barbarism.

The Roman emperor Constans II favored the heresy. St. Maximus attended the Lateran Council of 649, which condemned it. He was charged with conspiracy against the empire and exiled. Eventually, before he was sentenced to life imprisonment, his tongue and right hand (the two instruments he needed for teaching) were cut off. He died a short while later at the age of eighty-two. This was the abbot, now honored with the title "the Theologian," who wrote so simply but profoundly about the virtue of charity, or love.

Maximus began his first century with these words: "Charity is a good disposition of the soul, according to which one prefers no creature to the knowledge of God. It is impossible to attain a lasting possession of this charity if one has attachment to earthly things."

The relationship between faith, hope, and love was clear to him.

"Charity springs from the calm of detachment, detachment from hope in God, hope from patience and long-suffering; and these from all-embracing self-mastery; self-mastery from fear of God, fear of God from faith in the Lord."

If we have faith, we fear, that is, we rightly respect God and fear punishment. That fear helps us master our passions. Doing that means "enduring hardships with patience." It's then we discover "hope in God." And it's that hope that "separates the mind from every earthly attachment." That frees us to love God.

There's nothing better than that, the saint taught. It was for this that God created us. And the way we show that love for God, live that love, is by our love for others.

"He that loves me, says the Lord, will keep my commandments; and this is my commandment that you love one another. He therefore who does not love his neighbor does not keep the commandment. Nor is he that does not keep the commandment able to love the Lord."

Charity is not just "the distribution of money," St. Maximus stressed. It is "the distribution of the word of God" and "physical service of others." It's not just writing a check. It's sharing the Good News with others by what we say and what we do, and it is rolling up our sleeves and getting our hands dirty assisting others.

"He that genuinely renounces worldly affairs and unfeignedly [really] serves his neighbor out of charity, quickly is freed from every passion and is made partaker of divine charity and knowledge."

We come to know God better and experience his love to a greater degree, the more we serve others.

In his final point, number one hundred of the fourth set, St. Maximus acknowledged that "many have said much about charity." But this is the what he wanted to leave his readers with: "He . . . that possesses charity, possesses God himself, for God is charity."

It shouldn't be surprising that the themes St. Maximus returned to time and again are the same ones used by Thomas à Kempis in his classic the *Imitation of Christ.* The message doesn't change. Truth doesn't change.

Born around 1380 in Kempen, near Cologne, Germany, Thomas Hemerken is credited with writing one of the most popular books ever on spirituality (although over the years, some scholars have argued that he isn't the author). Its appeal has continued into our own time. St. Thomas More, St. Ignatius of Loyola, John Wesley, and Pope John XXIII are just some of the thousands who have publicly expressed their appreciation for this small book.

Ordained in 1413, Thomas à Kempis spent nearly his entire life in the cloister. He died in 1471. The *Imitation of Christ* was intended for his fellow religious. In it, he told them to "love all men for Jesus' sake, but Jesus for himself." Christ alone is to be loved with a special love, he said, "for he alone is the best and most faithful of friends."

In the same way, Thomas continued, don't wish to become the object of special praise or love, "for this belongs to God alone, who has none like himself." Thomas warned, "Do not desire that the heart of anyone be given wholly to yourself, and do not yield yourself wholly to the love of anyone; rather, let Jesus abide in you, and in every good person."

A young couple may want to be the whole world for each other, but they can't be. None of us can be everything for someone else. Anyone who expects that of us, who depends on that from us, is bound to be disappointed. Unless the love for God comes first, our love for another is hobbled. But through that love for God, our love for another can increase.

Love, Thomas wrote in what might called a hymn to this virtue, is a "mighty power, a great and complete good." It alone "lightens every burden, and makes the rough places smooth." It "bears every hardship as though it were nothing" and "renders all bitterness sweet and acceptable." The love of Jesus "inspires us to great deeds"; it "moves us always to desire perfection."

Thomas believed that "nothing is sweeter than love," nothing stronger, higher, wider, more pleasant, fuller, or "better in heaven or earth." That's because "love is born of God, and can rest only in God, above all created things."

Love "flies, runs and leaps for joy." It's "free and unrestrained." It "does not regard the gifts, but turns to the Giver of all good gifts." It "knows no limits, but ardently transcends all bounds."

Love "feels no burden, takes no account of toil, attempts things beyond its strength." Love "sees nothing as impossible, for it feels able to achieve all things."

But all this comes with a warning: "Whoever is not prepared to endure everything, and to stand firmly by the will of the Beloved, is not worthy to be called a lover. A lover must willingly accept every hardship and bitterness for the sake of his Beloved, and must never desert him because of adversity."

As we each draw closer to God, "the good and pleasant affection which you sometimes enjoy is the effect of God's grace in you," Thomas said; it is "a foretaste of your heavenly home." But we can't depend on that feeling. "Do not rely on it too much, for it comes and goes."

Thomas continued, "It is no illusion you are sometimes rapt out of yourself [we might say "on a cloud"], yet swiftly return to the usual trivial thoughts of men."

The priest counseled, "You may be sure the old Enemy is working by every means to frustrate your desire for good and to entice you away from every spiritual exercise of devotion." And "know that self-love does you more harm than anything else in the world."

We can't love God as we should, or love others, if we put ourselves first and if we put ourselves above others. "Humility is the surest road to love," Pope John XXIII noted in *Journal of a Soul,* a collection of his private writings. What makes his insight astounding is that Angelo Roncalli wrote those words in the summer of 1898 when he was a sixteen-year-old seminarian. "I will go to the school of Jesus," he said. "There I will learn to be always humble and loving."

The teenager prayed, "O good Jesus, enkindle in my heart your own burning love." A few weeks later, when his parish priest died, Angelo was "heartbroken" but took consolation "in obtaining, as a precious token of remembrance of my priest, his 'Imitation of Christ,' the same volume he had used every evening since his seminarist days."

The future pope noted, "To think he became holy, poring over this little book! This will always be my dearest book, and one of my most precious jewels!"

It was with this same earnestness that Angelo continuously examined his own life, admonishing himself that he had to "beware of talking about other people and above all sitting in judgment on Tom, Dick and Harry! It is just in these things that my old friend shows himself." What "old friend"? Self-love.

"With all these faults," he wrote the following year, "you [God] know also my desire to love and to make myself holy. So you must humiliate me, you must watch over me, you must sanctify me. Humility and love!"

After he was elected pope in 1958, the world would be astounded to see how humble this pontiff was. What people didn't realize was that for some six decades, he had intimately linked the virtues of love and humility and had worked constantly at fostering both.

It wasn't as if young Angelo had a premo-
nition he would become the successor of Peter.
Rather, he saw humility and love as the keys to
his future, whatever it might include. "Let us
then make a good start and work for love," he
wrote in 1900, "for this is what the Lord wills.
And working with Jesus of Nazareth in
prayerful seclusion, I will prepare myself to
accomplish more perfectly the mission which
awaits me, a mission of wisdom and love."

Two years later he wrote, "O Lord, do with
me whatever you will; I accept even death with
satisfaction and contentment, if that is your
wish. . . . But at least let me die in your holy love.
The strength you have given me to praise you
and to make you loved on earth I will use to love
you and praise you more ardently in heaven."

But death would mean judgment, he wrote.
And "even if I were to be pope, even if my
name were to be invoked and revered by all
and inscribed in marble monuments, I should
still have to stand before the divine judge, and
what should I be worth then? Not much."

What might have been frightening became
another reason to praise God as he realized
Jesus "took me, a country lad, from my home,
and with the affection of a loving mother . . .
has given me all I needed."

Angelo said, "In return for such tenderness,
he asks me anxiously only one thing: My son, do

you love me? Lord, Lord, how can I answer
you? See my tears, my throbbing heart, my
trembling lips, and the pen that slips from my
fingers. . . . What can I say? 'Lord, you know
that I love you.'"

Angelo's words are dramatic, but what he
wants is clear: to serve God through love. In
1961, he again quoted the words of Jesus' question and St. Peter's reply (John 21:15–19).
Then eighty and having been pontiff for three
years, he noted that it was upon this that the
church was built. Three times Jesus asks Peter
if he loves him. Three times Peter says he does.

"It is love, then, that matters," John
concluded.

"When I ponder this mystery of intimate love
between Jesus and his Vicar [that is, John himself, the current pope] I think what an honor and
what a joy it is for me, but at the same time what
a reason for shame for my own littleness and
worthlessness!" he wrote. "My life must be filled
with the love of Jesus and also with a great out-
pouring of goodness and sacrifice for individual
souls and for the whole of the world. For the
Gospel episode which proclaims the pope's love
for Jesus, and through him for souls, is but a
short step to the law of sacrifice."

The following year, some eight months
before his death, Pope John XXIII would open
the Second Vatican Council. On his private

retreat just before the first session, the theme would be the theological and cardinal virtues.

For Us Today

As a small tribute to St. Maximus and his style of writing, let's try a "half century" on love in our own time:

1. Every form of true love is a facet of God's love.

2. Our love for God is like no one else's. The love we show others reveals God to them in a way no one else can.

3. Love, by definition, cannot be selfish. Any selfishness is not love.

4. It's possible to have a twisted notion of love—to call something by that name that is really hurtful or harmful.

5. We hurt when our loved ones hurt, and our loved ones are going to hurt because we live in a world tainted by the consequences of sin and evil.

6. To avoid being hurt by not loving others is to hurt all the time.

7. It's easy to assume that we can't excel at love the way the saints did because we do not have their basic gifts, the same way most of us could never play professional sports. But each of us has the God-given potential to become a saint.

8. Some of the biggest sinners have become the biggest saints because they used the same energy and commitment they had put into being selfish and uncaring into loving and serving others.

9. We have to want to love in order to love. We have to want to grow in the virtue of love in order to increase our ability to love and be loved.

10. Most of us live small lives; we're asked to show love thousands of times in small ways. That's how we live out our vocation—the lifestyle and work to which God has called us.

11. We cannot and will not always feel love. That does not mean it no longer exists. Feeling can be a part of love, but it is not love. Love is infinitely more than a feeling.

12. God asks us to love for love's sake. That is, for *his* sake.

13. Love leads to the cross. The cross leads to resurrection. That is the Way.

14. Fasting and penance as signs of our love for God and as means to grow in virtue are unpopular, not because they aren't effective, but because they are hard.

15. All other virtues lead us to love. Without love, all other virtues are incomplete.

16. God never forces us to love him or our neighbor. To love is always a choice we have to make.

17. Just as it takes time and effort to grow in a loving relationship with our spouse or friend, our love for God requires those, too.

18. When we read "God so loved the world that he gave his only Son" (John 3:16), we can substitute "God so loved *me*. . . . "

19. Often people who don't recognize God's love have never felt his love for them through another human being.

20. We need to love ourselves without being selfish and without being self-centered.

21. On earth, we can never love God or others as much as we want to. We will always be imperfect lovers.

22. The more we come to know how much God loves us, the more meager our love for him appears.

23. We were created to love.

24. Today we can love more. We have only today. We have only right now.

25. Love begets love.

26. No one gets to the end of his or her life and says "I wish I had loved less."

27. Love is greater than death. Death does not stop love. We can continue to love those who have died, and they can continue to love us.

28. Anyone overflowing with Christian love is considered a fool by some and a sap by many.

29. Much of heaven is familiar to those who have loved well on earth.

30. We're called to love everyone, even those we won't ever like.

31. Love does more than let us see others through God's eyes. It lets us see God in theirs.

32. Every single person at our office or school, in our neighborhood or family, has the same craving: God's love. Most don't realize this is what they want. Too often we fail to give it to them.

33. The Good Shepherd said that if we love him, we must feed his sheep. Jesus promised to leave the ninety-nine and go after the one lost sheep. Sometimes the way he does that is to send us.

34. If praying and serving were easy, everyone would do them.

35. Sexual love has to do with the mind, the heart, and the soul as well as the body.

36. To love others means to recognize the pain their sin has caused them without being harsh to them or kind to their sin.

37. The more we love, the closer we move to becoming God's image.

38. We don't have to rely on words when we pray. At times, God asks us to be still and simply know that he is.

39. We must never lose sight of the fact that we are able to love only because God makes us able to love. If we become able to love more, it is because of him.

40. God has known each of us and loved each of us for all time with a love that has no end, no boundaries, no limits.

41. We can stop loving God, but we can never stop God from loving us.

42. Among the special ways God shows his love for us are Scripture and the sacraments. He extends to us an open invitation to join him in both.

43. Love sometimes means having to say we're sorry to God and to others. One of the best ways to do that is the sacrament of Reconciliation.

44. Love doesn't make a hard task pleasant. It gives us the reason for doing it.

45. Where we see joy, we'll find the root is love.

46. Love combined with humility lets us laugh at ourselves.

47. Just as, ultimately, we choose heaven or hell for ourselves, to a degree we do the same here and now. To choose love is to choose heaven.

48. Love never grows old, only deeper.

49. If we keep our eyes fixed on love, we can't lose our way.

50. Each of us is called to discover that God is love.

To Read More about It

Giuliana Cavallini, *Martin de Porres: Apostle of Charity* (St. Louis, Mo.: B. Herder Book Co., 1963).

John XXIII, *Journal of a Soul* (New York: McGraw-Hill, 1965).

C. S. Lewis, *The Four Loves* (New York: Harcourt Brace Jovanovich, 1960).

Thomas à Kempis, *Imitation of Christ*, trans. Leo Sherley-Price (Baltimore: Penguin, 1968).

CHAPTER 5

Prudence

In One Life

It all comes back to St. Gregory the Great.

When historians write of the development of nations during the Middle Ages, they point to the role the Catholic Church played. When they examine what the church did, they look to its bishops. When they study what shaped bishops' thought and actions during those centuries, they find a book called the *Pastoral Rule.* Gregory's *Pastoral Rule.*

Born in Rome around 540, Gregory came from a very wealthy, influential, and pious family. Two of his ancestors had been popes, including his great-great-grandfather, St. Felix III. In his early years, he received the finest education possible and then became a public official at a time when such a job involved much more than shuffling paper. During the previous century, the city had been sacked four times.

Gregory was about thirty when he was appointed prefect of the city, the highest civil office in Rome. As such, he was responsible for finances, food, defense, and policing. He was good at his job, and the people respected him and his abilities.

But Gregory felt he was being called to a very different life, a much simpler life. He resigned from his position and retired to his home, which he turned into a monastery under the care of a monk named Valentius, who became, Gregory wrote, "the superior of my monastery and of myself."

Gregory counted the few quiet years he spent as a monk the happiest of his life, but his talent and former prestige soon caught up with him. He was ordained one of Rome's seven deacons and sent as an ambassador to the Byzantine court in Constantinople, where he found the intrigue and exaggerated etiquette disgusting. He tried to balance the official demands of his job by living a somewhat monastic life with the several monks who had traveled there with him.

After seven years, he returned to Rome and was named abbot of his monastery. During this time, there were several severe outbreaks of plague, and the population was decimated. When

Pope Pelagius II died in early 590, the people rose up and chose Gregory to succeed him.

He didn't want to be pope. He didn't want to be a bishop. What he wanted was to remain a monk. Gregory had written about how difficult it was to be a bishop in the *Pastoral Rule*. It was his "defense" (his argument) to John, the archbishop of Ravenna, who had gently scolded him for trying to avoid office.

In the end, Gregory accepted the position, and his pontificate lasted for fourteen years. Because of what he accomplished during that time, the church later gave him the title "Gregory the Great." But the one he preferred, the one he chose, and the one used by popes since that time was "servant of the servants of God."

St. Gregory combined the practicality and order that had been the cornerstone of his career as a civil leader with the ascetic spirituality that had been his vocation as a monk. He deposed one of Rome's archdeacons who was corrupt, forbade the charging of fees for ordinations and burials, urged the liberal treatment of servants, and ordered that money be advanced to those in financial straits. His huge charities saved countless Romans from starvation. He would not allow Jews to be deprived of their synagogues.

When a Lombard army appeared at Rome's gates in 593, Pope Gregory went out to meet with the king and convinced him to leave the city alone in exchange for an annual tribute. When the Lombards and Byzantines couldn't settle their differences, he negotiated his own treaty with them, getting a special truce for Rome and its surrounding area.

He sent missionaries to England and is credited (perhaps incorrectly) with compiling a collection of church music now known as Gregorian chant. For several centuries, his was the last word on theology, and his *Pastoral Rule* was presented to all new bishops.

Clearly, his words apply to anyone in authority: pastor, parent, boss, or teacher. Gregory's practical wisdom, his prudence, can be found throughout his book. And, more impressive, his contemporaries said he applied that prudence in his own life. The epitaph on his tomb at St. Peter's Basilica reads, "After having conformed all his actions to his doctrines, the great consul of God went to enjoy eternal triumphs."

The *Pastoral Rule* is divided into four parts. The first looks at the difficulties of the pastoral office and the requirements it places on someone called to it. The second examines the inner and outer life of a good pastor. The third explains the best way to teach the various classes of people a pastor is called upon to rule. And the fourth reminds the pastor of how he should be mindful of his own weaknesses.

In the opening chapter, Gregory warns his readers: "Although those who have no knowledge of the powers of drugs shrink from giving themselves out as physicians of the flesh, people who are utterly ignorant of spiritual precepts are often not afraid of professing themselves to be physicians of the heart." Anyone can claim to be a spiritual director, a mentor, or a guru, and in fact some "reign by their own conceit, not by the will of the Supreme Ruler." These people "are sustained by no virtues, are not divinely called, but being inflamed by their own cupidity [greed], they seize rather than attain supreme rule." If they have no spiritual foundation, no spiritual life, they are "the blind leading the blind," guiding others and themselves "into the pit."

Equally dangerous and damaging, Gregory said, is the spiritual leader who has knowledge of right and wrong but leads a corrupt life. "For no one does more harm in the Church than he, who having the title or rank of holiness, acts evilly." He or she "muddies the waters," and that person's followers, while thirsting for truth, end up trying to drink mud.

Gregory knew that "often it happens when a man undertakes the care of government, his heart is distracted with a diversity of things, and as his mind is divided among many interests and becomes confused, he finds himself unfitted for any of them." (How many of us have felt that same way with the demands of life in general?)

The solution? "This is why a certain wise man gives cautious warning, saying, 'My son, meddle not with many matters'; for, in fact, the mind cannot possibly concentrate on the pursuit of any one matter when it is divided among many." A mind so caught up in external details, Gregory said, is like someone "so preoccupied during a journey as to forget what [the] destination was."

Who, then, is a wise ruler, a good ruler? The one who devotes himself or herself "entirely to setting an ideal of living." One who is "quickly moved by a compassionate heart to forgive, yet never so diverted from perfect rectitude as to forgive beyond what is proper." (And certainly prudence would dictate what degree of forgiveness is proper.)

"Everyone should wisely assess himself," Gregory wrote, "lest he dare to take on the role of governing, while vice still reigns in him to his condemnation; a man who is debased by his own guilt must not intercede for the faults of others."

Who wouldn't be a good leader? The person so "oppressed by the darkness of the present life" that he "does not know where to direct the steps of his conduct." The person who, "through infirmity of purpose, is unable to follow persistently the way of life" that she sees. The one "incapable of discernment," unable (or unwilling) to "elect virtue and reject sin." Those who, "disliking to be considered dull, often busy themselves with a variety of inquisitions, more than is needful, and fall into error by their excessive subtlety." In a word, hairsplitters.

The one who would make a poor leader, Gregory wrote, is "wholly unable to walk in the way of God and is entirely bereft of all share in good deeds." She is "weighted down by the burden of earthly cares" and so "never looks up to the things that are above, but is wholly intent on what is underfoot in the lowest sphere."

This is the person "whose natural disposition does, indeed shine forth unto the knowledge of truth, but is obscured by carnal works." He once was "capable of a nice discrimination of what was right," but his vision has been "obscured by the habit of evil deeds." ("We anoint our eyes with salve for seeing," the pope said, "when we assist the eye of our understanding with the medicine of good works, so that we may perceive the brightness of true light.") The poor leader is blinded "by the arrogant assumption of wisdom or righteousness." Gregory said that "when a man understands he is foolish and a sinner his faculty of thought grasps the knowledge of the interior light."

In addition, Gregory wrote, a poor ruler would be one "constantly dominated by wantonness of the flesh" or possessing a "mind . . . ravaged by avarice." It is one who, if not "actually given to baseness, is yet weighed down beyond measure by the constant thought of it." Though such a person "is not carried away by evil deeds, his mind is ravished with the pleasure of lechery, without any stings of repugnance."

Conversely, a good bishop "should be discreet in keeping silence and profitable in speech, lest he utter what should be kept secret, or keep secret what should be uttered." So, "when the ruler prepares to speak, he must bear in mind to exercise a studious caution in his speech, for if his discourse, hastily given, be ill-ordered, the hearts of his hearers may be stricken by the wound of error, and when, perhaps, he wishes to appear wise, he will by his lack of wisdom sever the bond of unity."

He added, "Rulers must also see to it with careful concern that not only should nothing evil proceed from their lips, but that not even what is proper be said in excess or in a slovenly manner. Often the force of what is said is wasted, when it is enfeebled in the hearts of the hearers by a careless and offensive torrent of words."

Being a wise leader is a balancing act, the saint said. "Let the ruler not relax the care of the inner life by preoccupying himself with external matters, nor should his solicitude with the inner life bring neglect of the external, lest, being engrossed with what is external, he be ruined inwardly, or being preoccupied with what concerns only his inner self, he does not bestow on his neighbors the necessary external care."

He reminded his readers, "Doctrine taught does not penetrate the minds of the needy, if a compassionate heart does not commend it to the hearts of the hearers." But "the seed of the word does germinate properly when the kindness of a preacher waters it in the hearer's heart." And "the ruler should not be zealous to please men, yet should give heed to what ought to please them."

The wise leader "should also understand that vices commonly masquerade as virtues. Often, for instance, a miser passes himself off as frugal, while one who is wasteful conceals his character when he calls himself generous. Often inordinate laxity is believed to be kindness, and unbridled anger passes as the virtue of spiritual zeal." That's why "it is necessary that the ruler of souls discern with care and vigilance virtues from vices."

In the same way, the ruler knows "at times the faults of subjects must be prudently overlooked, but they should be given to understand that they are being overlooked." Indeed, "the prudence required of the ruler" is knowing when to be rigorous and when to be gentle, when to correct and when to not ignore but, for a time, allow.

That describes Gregory's life. Prudence — the ability to apply knowledge, experience, and general wisdom to specific situations and people — made him an appreciated and valuable public official. Prudence led him from that job and lifestyle into the monastery. Prudence told him to accept the pontificate and allowed him to govern the church wisely.

It was not his intellect, as keen as it might have been, that, years after his death, earned him the title "St. Gregory the Great." It was his compassionate wisdom that led to his canonization and that shaped the church and centuries of its leaders.

In Scripture

There are plenty of prudent people in Scripture: Abraham, who could argue prudently, even with God (Genesis 18:16–33); Joseph, who managed Egypt's grain supply through seven years of famine (Genesis 47:13–26); the exemplary wife who knows how to care for her family (Proverbs 31:10–31); the servant in Jesus' parable who will be given his "allowance of food at the proper time" (Luke 12:42).

Prudence has to do with bringing broad, general, moral knowledge to bear on a particular situation. It's closely related to wisdom, which is the highest and most essential knowledge, namely, knowledge of God. That's why any discussion on prudence in Scripture needs to begin with a look at wisdom.

In some ways, wisdom in the Old Testament had a rather everyday quality. It was a simple teaching. Anyone with any sense would want it because it was valuable; anyone who didn't want it was a fool. But wisdom also came to be understood as something much more than that. It was a powerful gift from God and even *of* God.

As with any people, over time the Israelites began to follow a set of "rules" that were based on human experience. We still do that. In fact, some of those recorded by the chosen people are very familiar in our own age: for example, "Pride goes before a fall" or "If you play with fire, you're going to get burned" (see Proverbs 16:18; 6:27).

The Israelites collected their bits of wisdom and handed them down from generation to generation. They can be found especially in Proverbs, a book that holds up remarkably well in describing what we humans are like, warts and all.

The Jews also borrowed from their neighbors. If the Egyptians or the Babylonians had some practical knowledge, the people of Israel were happy to include it. But when they did that, they made that wisdom their own by giving it a religious connotation and tying it in with their faith in Yahweh.

An Egyptian proverb might have been addressed only to the upper crust, the scribes and officials. When it became Jewish, it was applied to every Jew. It wasn't just the elite who needed to love and pursue wisdom; it was each Jew because each had the same covenant relationship with God.

Wisdom was seen as a gift from the Creator, and the Hebrew law offered wisdom. That meant that, in order to become wise, a person needed to learn not just what human nature teaches—what any people of any culture over time figure out—but what Jewish Scripture teaches.

For a time, the two concepts of wisdom, common sense and gift from God, were at work side by side. Eventually "religious wisdom" became dominant and absorbed what we might call "practical wisdom." This meant the Jews believed wisdom was both a grace from God and the result of experience and learning. God granted great wisdom to leaders, such as Solomon, and it was available to anyone willing to pursue it. Who could receive it? Holy souls (Wisdom 7:27) who stood in God's favor

(Ecclesiastes 2:26) and loved him (Sirach 1:10). To obtain wisdom, then, one needed to pray (Wisdom 7:7; 8:21) and needed to be taught (Wisdom 6:9).

Why would a person want to be wise? Because to choose wisely in everyday life was to choose true happiness.

The Jews also considered ability with a craft, any manual skill, a kind of wisdom. An experienced and prudent counselor was said to have wisdom, as was an elder. The scribes, those who knew the Law well, were wise; so were "sages," a class probably identical to the scribes. Along with the prophets and priests, they were the upper class and most likely were the ones who collected the wisdom sayings and used them to teach others.

They taught that Yahweh was wise, but they also sometimes pictured wisdom itself as a distinct entity with an existence of its own. In Proverbs, wisdom is personified as a female preacher who speaks of her own origins; she was at God's side when he created the universe. The book of Sirach describes how she went forth from the Creator and, at his request, came to stay in Israel, where she grew and bore fruit. In the book of Wisdom, she leads the Jews in their activities, preserves them, and rescues them. She makes them friends of God and of the prophets. She is immutable and all-powerful. She lives with God, and God loves her.

Why did they personify divine wisdom? Perhaps as a way of affirming both the utter transcendence of God and the evidence of divine wisdom in the world (Wisdom 7:22–8:1). Wisdom is seen as an intermediary, an emissary of God. (In similar ways, the Old Testament speaks of the Word, the Spirit, and, sometimes, the angel of God.) Such language in the Old Testament paved the way for the full revelation of God as Father, Son, and Spirit in the New Testament.

There Jesus is the Word and wisdom of God. Luke tells us that Jesus, born a human, grew "in wisdom and in years, and in divine and human favor" (Luke 2:52). Once an adult and preaching with authority, he is credited with religious and moral wisdom, as well as the wisdom of the scribes. (The local folks around Nazareth can't figure out how he learned so much! After all, they knew him when. . . .)

In a passage beginning with Matthew 11:18, what Jesus does—his works—are compared to the works of wisdom. Jesus himself uses expressions from the Old Testament that describe the relationship of the divine wisdom of God to humans.

Paul takes specific traits of wisdom as shown in the Old Testament, especially the book of Wisdom, and transfers them as attributes of the divine wisdom in Jesus. He is the image of the invisible God. The firstborn of all creation. Through him everything came to be. We exist through him. It is because of him everything continues to exist. (See Colossians 1:15–18.)

But it is the evangelist John who really stresses that there is a correspondence between the divine wisdom of the Old Testament and the Christ of the New. In his prologue, John relies on wisdom literature when writing of Jesus, whom he calls the "Word" (in Greek, *logo*s).

In the Gospel itself, John notes that Jesus, like divine wisdom, has come forth from God; has been beloved by God from the very beginning; has been given all things by God; lives in intimate union with God; and is initiated into the knowledge of God. Jesus, like wisdom, has been sent into the world in order to redeem it; makes his home among humans and in doing so draws them to the love of God; lives in those who love him; and so establishes an inner relationship between God and humans.

Then, too, in order for someone to come to Jesus or to wisdom, he or she first needs God's grace. An individual's destiny is determined by the attitude he or she has toward Jesus or wisdom because Jesus (or wisdom) maintains life like God himself. So the person who observes the commandments of wisdom and of Jesus obtains eternal life.

Again, none of this points to a "wisdom goddess" or a fourth person in God but shows that the wisdom of God spoken of in the Hebrew Scriptures is revealed in Christ in the New Testament. To follow Christ is to follow wisdom because the wisdom of God lives in Christ, who is God.

God is divine wisdom. Christ is God. So Christ is also wisdom.

If prudence and wisdom were concepts used throughout the Old and New Testaments, so was the idea of folly, or foolishness. A fool was one who refused to (or was unable to) accept instruction. He didn't learn from experience and didn't behave according to the dictates of the community.

A fool hated wisdom and discipline (Proverbs 1:7); laughed at warnings (15:5); despised being corrected (12:1) or taught (23:9); and didn't listen to good advice (12:15). It wasn't even possible to beat sense into him: "A rebuke strikes deeper into a discerning person than a hundred blows into a fool" (17:10).

It's easy to imagine the fools in the Israelite community two or three thousand years ago because there are the same kinds of people in our own time, in our own communities. We know what fools are like. We come across them daily. (And, truth be told, sometimes we act foolishly.)

Then or now? The fool lacks prudence when dealing with others and speaks without thinking (Proverbs 10:14) and at the wrong time (20:19). He gives an answer before he has time to hear the complete question (18:13), and his manners are, well, awful (Sirach 21:22–24).

Then *and* now.

But foolishness to the Hebrews was more than simply ignoring common sense and community decency. Since the fool hates all kinds of instruction, he certainly isn't going to learn religious truths or follow moral guidelines. He isn't going to obey Yahweh's commandments. To sin, then, was to be foolish. That's why the person with any sense avoids the company of fools since they can only bring trouble (Proverbs 13:20; 27:3).

In the New Testament, the foolish are sometimes those who don't "get it," who don't follow the wisdom of Christ's teaching. Like the man who built his house on sand, they do not build their existence on the firm foundation of Christ's teaching and so are swept away by the storms of life (Matthew 7:26–27). Or, like the five foolish virgins, they are caught unprepared for the bridegroom's return and so fail to enter the banquet of everlasting life (Matthew 25:1–13).

But sometimes the New Testament says that the very followers of Christ are the real fools. So

Paul exhorts the Corinthians to "become fools" (1 Corinthians 3:18–19). He invites them (and us) to follow the foolishness of the cross. "For Jews demand signs and Greeks desire wisdom, but we proclaim Christ crucified, a stumbling block to Jews and foolishness to Gentiles, but to those who are the called, both Jews and Greeks, Christ the power of God and the wisdom of God. For God's foolishness is wiser than human wisdom, and God's weakness is stronger than human strength" (1 Corinthians 1:22–25).

The preaching of the cross, the preaching of Christ crucified, seems foolish to the world. And one who hears that preaching is forced to choose between the wisdom of the world and the foolishness of the cross. The way of the world seems wise, conventional, understandable, safe. The way of the cross seems risky, unknown, incomprehensible. The world offers the tidy security of self-seeking, while the cross opens the uncharted risk of self-giving.

All we know for sure is that to follow the way of the cross is to follow the foolishness of God, which is the foolishness of love. In that foolishness alone lies the promise of true wisdom.

Down through the Ages

We may think of discretion as only "the better part of valor." And one who is discreet as the person who simply has the ability to maintain secrets.

Some sixteen centuries ago, the desert father and monk John Cassian explained that "the gift of discretion is no earthly thing and no slight matter, but the greatest prize of divine grace." Where he used that word, we could easily substitute *prudence* or *wisdom*.

Cassian (ca. 360–433) wrote about this virtue in his "Conferences on the Egyptian Monks." Never canonized in the West, he is considered a saint in the Eastern church. A good storyteller, he explains to his listeners (his readers) that he plans to show how "the fathers" (those who have gone before) valued this virtue and then to offer "some ancient and modern shipwrecks and mischances of various people who were destroyed and hopelessly ruined because they paid little attention to it." This is "no ordinary virtue nor one which can be freely gained by merely human efforts." No, we need to be "aided by the Divine blessing."

Why would his fellow monks, or we, want it? "Unless a monk has pursued it with all zeal, and secured a power of discerning with unerring judgment the spirits that rise up in him, he is sure to go wrong, as if in the darkness of night and dense blackness, and not merely to fall down dangerous pits and precipices, but also make frequent mistakes in matters that are plain and straightforward."

Without prudence, we make the wrong choices in our lives. Big ones and little ones. Wisdom is light, and without it we are "full of darkness." Anyone "not fortified by sound judgment and knowledge or deceived by some error and presumption" stumbles in the dark. "For no one can doubt that when the judgment of our heart goes wrong, and is overwhelmed by the night of ignorance, our thoughts and deeds, which are the result of deliberation and discretion, must be involved in the darkness of still greater sins." Or, more crudely put, at first we may only stub our toe a few times, but eventually we will walk off a cliff.

But "herein lies wisdom, herein lies intelligence and understanding without which our inward house cannot be built, nor can spiritual riches be gathered together": "Do everything with counsel." Think! Ask those who know! Learn! "No virtue can possibly be perfectly acquired or continued without the grace of discretion." "It is discretion which leads a fearless monk by fixed stages to God."

Discretion — prudence, wisdom — is the virtue that "preserves" the other virtues in us and keeps them intact, so "one may ascend with less weariness to the extreme summit of perfection." And without them, "those who toil most willingly" can't reach "its heights." Here's the deal, Cassian told the monks: "Discretion is the mother of all virtues, as well as their guardian and regulator." If we want to grow spiritually, if we want to cultivate other virtues, we have to pay close attention to prudence. Without it, no matter how virtuous we consider ourselves, we may simply be stupid, or worse. What we may think is a holy act may be wholly ridiculous.

Cassian gave the example of two monks setting off into the desert with no food or water. They ignored common sense because, they maintained, "God would provide." Later, near dead from hunger and thirst, they were found by members of a ferocious tribe who, amazingly, offered them help. One of the monks gratefully accepted the aid and lived. The other "refused . . . because it was offered to him by men [rather than directly by God] and died of starvation." Cassian pointed out that both monks had made the same original mistake but that only one had sense enough — had discretion — to correct it when the opportunity presented itself. (Or to see God did provide, but not in the way they had expected.)

It is only with the God-given gift of wisdom that we can recognize "a devil in the brightness of an angelic form." With discretion, "the fountain head and the root of all virtues," we can tell whether a thought or action, a plan or goal, "is genuine and from God" or "spurious and from the devil."

But how can we receive this virtue, and how do we nurture it within ourselves? It's "only secured by true humility," Cassian said. We have to be willing to accept instruction, to listen to others, to not be a know-it-all. God's Word and his wisdom can come to us through the Christian community, through the mystical body of Christ.

The author gave the example of St. Paul's conversion (Acts 9:1–19). Christ appeared to Paul but didn't give him instructions directly. Rather, he sent Paul to learn from an elder in the fledgling community. In the same way, we, too, can learn from elders who display Christian wisdom. We can come to discern how to avoid being injured by "either extreme." Cassian reminded his readers of the old saying "Extremes meet."

He gave the example of gluttony and excessive fasting, of being too fond of sleep and too fond of all-night prayer vigils that keep one from sleeping. Either way, a monk ends up unable to think clearly, Cassian said. Either way, he becomes careless, negligent, and open to temptation. Prudence helps us live with "due moderation." It shows us how to "walk between the two extremes."

If Cassian's words seem like good advice to us, they had the same effect on the great theologian Thomas Aquinas, too. St. Thomas (1225–74) read Cassian daily, but when he wrote about prudence, he quoted St. Augustine, St. Ambrose, and Aristotle.

In his *Summa Theologiae*, St. Thomas reminded his readers it was the bishop of Hippo who said, "Prudence is the knowledge of what to seek and what to avoid." It is "love discerning aright that which helps from that which hinders us in tending to God."

In the same way, St. Thomas quoted St. Augustine's teacher, St. Ambrose: "Prudence is concerned with the quest of truth, and fills us with the desire of fuller knowledge." With prudence, we learn to recognize how much more we have to learn.

St. Thomas also noted that according to "the philosopher" Aristotle, "prudence is right reason applied to action." It is "wisdom about human affairs," "wisdom for man," but "not wisdom absolutely." And, again quoting St. Augustine, it's "the science of what to desire and what to avoid."

It is a virtue, St. Thomas said. And like all virtues, it's "that which make its possessor good, and his work good likewise." Far from being only abstract, prudence directs our actions. It makes us hunger for what will truly satisfy us and avoid what will end up making us sick.

This virtue "applies universal principles to the particular conclusions of practical matters." What does that mean? Well, for example, the commandment to honor one's parents is a universal principle. How to correctly apply that with regard to our own mother and father is governed by prudence.

Prudence is the gift, St. Thomas said, that allows us to determine the right path. It's what lets us distinguish between bravery and foolhardiness. Between cowardice or common sense. It was Shakespeare who wrote, "The better part of valor is discretion." Perhaps to put it more accurately, we should say discretion allows us to choose the better part of valor, whatever that part may be in our particular circumstances at that particular time.

St. Thomas taught that there is also false prudence, true-but-imperfect prudence, and true prudence. False prudence, he said, is what we possess when we're good at being bad. (We're a prudent robber if we take all the steps we can to avoid getting caught.) True-but-imperfect prudence helps us make the right decision, but then we fail by not carrying it out. (We vow to lose weight but buy a cheesecake the next time we're at the grocery store.) True prudence makes the same initial decision but then "takes counsel."

(We make the same vow and then search out and follow the advice of others who have been successful at losing weight.)

St. Thomas's examples show that prudence doesn't only apply to what we would call our "spiritual life." After all, it—along with justice, fortitude, and temperance—was a virtue the Greeks admired. But, when it comes to our spiritual life, "no man has grace unless he be virtuous," and "no man can be virtuous without prudence." In fact, "the virtues must . . . be connected together so that whoever has one has all."

It takes "experience and time" to acquire prudence, St. Thomas explained. That's why "it cannot be in the young, neither in habit nor in act." He admitted, "On the other hand, gratuitous prudence is caused by divine infusion." God's grace can give wisdom to anyone at any age.

It could be said prudence isn't instinctual. It's "not inherited from nature" but "acquired by discovery through experience, or through teaching." But then, it could be countered that we are naturally inclined to seek what makes us happy. And prudence shows the way to happiness, that is, to God.

St. Teresa of Ávila (1515–82), the great reformer of the Carmelites in Spain, put prudence (common sense) before piety when it came to any young woman who was interested in joining her new, stricter convents. "Even though our Lord should give this young girl devotion and teach her contemplation, if she has no sense she never will come to have any," Teresa wrote, "and instead of use to the community, she will be a burden."

And more bluntly: "May God preserve us from stupid nuns."

Small wonder St. Teresa valued prudence. It was a virtue she needed in her delicate role of pointing out where some convents had grown lax in their religious fervor (being more like resorts than houses of prayer) and beginning new communities that would follow a more austere and ascetic life.

Needless to say, she and her ideas weren't always welcomed with open arms—not by nuns, not by clerics, not by government officials. Often she relied on discretion, not to water down the message she was giving, but to determine the method in which she gave it. While she herself was a mystic who had a powerful and personal relationship with God that included visions, she never lost sight of the need to reach out to others in the most practical ways possible. In the ways that would be most effective when dealing specifically with them.

When Teresa was appointed prioress of a convent that hadn't reformed and had no interest in doing so, she told the sisters she wasn't going to force anything on them. They had nothing to fear from her. She said, "I come solely to serve you." Over time, she won their confidence and was able to initiate a number of changes.

Wisdom helped Teresa understand that some nuns weren't ready to answer the call to the stricter observance she was promoting and others simply didn't have that particular vocation. It also gave her the ability to stand up to higher authorities in church and state when that was called for. Her discretion, one biographer later noted, told her when to use her charm and when to use her intelligence in dealing with those who at first opposed her or simply dismissed her.

It was true wisdom, Teresa knew, that helped her push aside "a thousand fears and considerations of human prudence" that were telling her God's will couldn't be done.

It was true wisdom that made her observe that we "should not take for granted that every little fancy we may have is a vision." Sometimes our ideas are foolish, and following them would be, too. She counseled, "The vision when true will make itself understood." Waiting to see if our "fancy"—our idea, our plan—is from the Holy Spirit spares us a lot of trouble and keeps us from looking foolish to others.

It was prudence, too, that gave Teresa the ability to admit when she was mistaken. For instance, a woman once suggested a monastery be founded in a particular area, but Teresa was strongly against it for a number of valid reasons. But, Teresa said, "I laid the matter before learned men and my confessor" and "they told me I was in the wrong." They pointed out she didn't have the right to stop "the foundation of a house wherein our Lord might be so well served." She began the community, and it prospered. "One day in prayer, after Communion," she wrote, "I heard our Lord say that he would be greatly honored in that house." She tried to teach her sisters the same attitude, encouraging them to "go always for direction" from the "learned," because that was how they would "find the way of perfection in discretion and truth."

Perhaps the key to Teresa's wisdom was that despite being a brilliant mystic, she never failed to remember that "God walks among the pots and pans." She understood it's there, in everyday life, that we need the virtue of prudence to choose what leads us toward him and to avoid what leads us away.

For Us Today

It may seem hard to muster much enthusiasm for prudence these days. The very name sounds old-fashioned and, well, prudish. But if we consider it carefully, we may find that prudence answers a need that's especially evident in our modern mind-set.

We tend to be pretty pragmatic. We don't have a lot of patience for long theories and explanations. We like to get down to brass tacks. We're eager to "walk the walk," not just "talk the talk." In a word, we want to know what we should do.

It's not a new question. It's the same one the crowds asked John the Baptist: "What then should we do?" (Luke 3:10). The same one they asked Jesus: "What must we do to perform the works of God?" (John 6:28).

It's not an easy question. Oh, it may be simple enough to memorize the Ten Commandments (or look them up in Exodus 20:1–17 or Deuteronomy 5:6–21). And it's true that they do serve as rules to govern our life and action. But how do they apply in this situation, in the particular circumstances of our life right now? "Honor your father and your mother" seems clear enough, until one is faced with an alcoholic parent who refuses to admit the problem or an elderly parent who may need the care of a nursing home.

The rich young man who came up to Jesus with the question "What must I do to inherit eternal life?" was well aware of the Ten Commandments (Mark 10:17–22). In fact he said, "I have kept all these since my youth." He knew the commandments, but he wanted to know what to *do*. How to apply those rules, how to translate them into a plan of action for himself then and there. What, he asked, are they calling me to?

Jesus, the very Word and wisdom of God, could apply those general rules to the particular situation of the young man. He could look at the rules but also look at the young man "with love" and see how the two were connected (or should be connected). He could see the way that would lead to joy: "You lack one thing; go, sell what you own, and give the money to the poor, and you will have treasure in heaven; then come, follow me."

Jesus gave the invitation to joy — suggested the perfect fit between those laws and that life — but the young man did not accept it. In one of the saddest passages in all of Scripture, we're told that the young man "went away grieving, for he had many possessions."

What is the invitation that Jesus gives to us? What should we do? How shall we find our way to joy? We ask those questions on many different levels, in many different circumstances. Sometimes, it's a fundamental decision about a career or vocation; sometimes it's a quandary about how to approach a friend or a spouse to seek reconciliation; sometimes it's a moral dilemma about the right course of action in a certain circumstance. How do we decide? How do we know?

Prudence is the virtue that helps us. It lets us put our decisions in perspective by reminding us that the goal of all our actions is life and friendship with God. From the inner core, or center, of that friendship, we determine what to do. Our decisions are not just matters of the head but also matters of the heart if prudence, as Augustine says, is a kind of love.

Prudence doesn't give us instant answers. Like all of the virtues, it's a kind of habit, or art. And like every habit, it's something we have to learn and get better at with practice. So wisdom is the traditional possession not of the young but of the old.

How do we grow in wisdom or prudence? Scripture says, first, that we should ask for it. "I prayed, and understanding was given me; I called on God, and the spirit of wisdom came to me" (Wisdom 7:7). To ask for something is to admit that we don't yet possess it. In this case, it means we have the humility to recognize that we haven't got all the answers, that our opinions and judgments are not synonymous with gospel truth. We need to seek counsel. If Paul, after his direct experience of Jesus, still needed the ministry and counsel of others, how much more do we? Once we've asked for prudence (or as we continue to ask for it), we need to practice it. Like throwing a football or baking a soufflé, it's not something we're likely to "get right" the first time we try it.

If prudence means "applying universal principles to particular situations," we've got to try out a few such applications. It's not an easy thing to do. And, like other hard things, we sometimes try to dodge it altogether. One popular evasion is legalism. We simply invoke "the letter of the law" without looking at the particular circumstances of the individual case. We can then wrap ourselves in the righteousness of "orthodoxy" or "the law" (or even "the rubrics" in liturgical discussions) and pretend that the universal rule needs no interpretation. It must apply in the same way in all circumstances.

This was the approach of the Pharisees, for example, when they criticized Jesus for allowing his disciples to pick and eat the grain as they walked through the fields on the Sabbath (Matthew 12:1–8). By the letter of the law, such activity was defined as work and, as such, was forbidden. Jesus' response was to give examples of how a universal law might apply (or not apply) in certain circumstances: "Have you not read what David did when he and his companions were hungry? He entered the house of God and ate the bread of the Presence, which it was not lawful for him or his companions to eat, but only for the priests."

Prudence must determine how the law applies in each circumstance. If the law applied in exactly the same way at all times, this virtue would be unnecessary.

Another way to sidestep the difficult work of prudential judgments is a kind of liberalism that simply ignores the law altogether. It's saying our circumstances are so special that the law is rendered irrelevant. Whatever the state or the church requires is simply set aside as having no bearing on our particular action.

An example of this attitude can also be found among the Pharisees. Some of them thought that the requirements of the Fourth Commandment regarding respect for and support of one's parents were simply irrelevant to one who dedicated his goods to God: "You have a fine way of rejecting the commandment of God in order to keep your tradition!" Jesus scolded them. "For Moses said, 'Honor your father and your mother.' . . . But you say that if anyone tells father or mother, 'Whatever support you might have had from me is Corban' (that is, an offering to God) — then you no longer permit doing anything for a father or mother, thus making void the word of God through your tradition that you have handed on. And you do many things like this" (Mark 7:9–13).

All this means the virtue, or art, of prudence is not ready-made. We learn it only after a good deal of work, a good deal of patience, and many mistakes. Practicing prudence might be compared to learning to kayak down a white-water river. The novice has to keep an eye on both sides, paddling a course that avoids running aground while also missing the rocks. If she clings to either shore, she may feel safe and secure, but she'll never learn the sport.

In the same way, the prudent individual plots a course through the rapids of daily life, keeping one eye on the rocky bank of universal principles and the other on the muddy shore of particular circumstances. If she gets stuck on either side, if she simply clings to stony principles or sinks into the easy ooze of particular circumstances, she may feel safe and secure (self-righteous or self-satisfied), but she isn't practicing the art of prudence. It's only if she's daring enough and trusting enough to stay out in the river that she learns.

To carry the metaphor one step further, just as the kayaker who continues down the river may eventually find her way to the sea, so the one who continues to practice prudence will find her way to the infinite ocean of divine love. Following day by day, act by act, stroke by stroke, she'll find the love that chooses wisely between "that which helps and that which hinders us in tending to God."

To Read More about It

Rosemary Broughton, *Praying with Teresa of Ávila* (Winona, Minn.: St. Mary's Press, 1990).

John C. Cavadini, ed., *Gregory the Great: A Symposium* (Notre Dame, Ind.: University of Notre Dame Press, 1996).

Daniel Mark Nelson, *The Priority of Prudence: Virtue and Natural Law in Thomas Aquinas and the Implications for Modern Ethics* (University Park, Pa.: Pennsylvania State University Press, 1992).

Daniel Westberg, *Right Practical Reason: Aristotle, Action, and Prudence in Aquinas* (New York: Oxford University Press, 1994).

CHAPTER 6

Justice

In One Life

The rich and powerful leaders of El Salvador welcomed the appointment of Oscar Romero as archbishop of San Salvador in February 1977. At a time when that country was being rocked by workers and organizers demanding change, members of the oligarchy—the small ruling class—were certain he would not make waves. They assumed, at best, he was one of them; at worst, he could be controlled or would control the people by stressing a passive Christianity.

They were wrong.

It's not hard to understand why they made that mistake. Bishop Romero had a reputation and a talent for making peace, he tended to have a conservative outlook, and he had links to the Salvadoran rulers. Born in 1917 in

Cuidad Barrios, a city that borders Honduras, Romero was the son of a telegraph operator and a homemaker. Bright and conscientious, he entered the seminary in San Salvador and was ordained in 1942. The next year he went to Rome for further studies.

The young priest then returned to his homeland and began parish work. In 1970, he was ordained a bishop and went to work for Archbishop Luis Chavez in San Salvador. Four years later, he was named bishop of the diocese of Santiago de Maria, where the people to whom he ministered had good jobs and hefty incomes. What he failed to recognize were the other Salvadorans—the many citizens who lived in extreme poverty and worked under brutal conditions.

During those years, for the first time, the government and major private businesses went after not only the secular institutions and organizations that backed change (meaning the ones that backed the rights of the working class) but also the Catholic Church. Action was directed against the priests, religious, and lay ministers who dared to side with the *campesinos*, the farm workers. The San Salvador archdiocesan printing press, a Catholic bookshop, and the Central American University had become the targets for bombs. Six priests had been expelled from the country, and Archbishop Chavez had been attacked in the media for allowing and encouraging "communistic sermons."

Some members of the clergy were disappointed—and worried—when Oscar Romero was chosen to succeed Chavez. They, like the civil and business leaders, could see him working hand in hand with the powerful in the kind of unjust church-state relationship that, sadly, sometimes flourished during feudal times. The priests noticed, and were heartened, when Romero took over as archbishop in a simple, private ceremony to which the government had not been invited.

Less than a week after the archbishop assumed office, security forces and the military gunned down demonstrators who had gathered in a plaza to protest what they saw as fraud in the recent election of General Carlos Humberto Romero as president. A new popular organization, which would become known for its radicalism and aggressiveness, was born: the Popular Leagues of the 28th of February.

Within that single month, three new key players were in place: General Romero, who had been the minister of defense and public security; Archbishop Romero, considered a conservative churchman; and the Popular Leagues. In the weeks that followed, a priest was arrested and tortured, a house of lay workers was raided, and eight priests were refused permission to enter the country. On March 12, Father Rutilio Grande and two companions, a boy and an old man, were killed on their way to Mass in the village where Father Grande had been born and where he served as a parish priest. He was to be the first of many priests killed by Salvadoran forces. His murder was seen as more than just the death of a member of the clergy but as an attack on the pastoral approach the church was adopting at that time: a preferential option for the poor.

Archbishop Romero would later recall many times that the killing of Father Grande was a crucial moment in his life, in his "conversion" toward actively and fearlessly promoting justice for the poorest members of his country. Father Grande had been a good friend. He had been someone the archbishop had greatly admired.

Other deaths followed to the point that Archbishop Romero commented, "It was my lot to go on claiming dead bodies. These days I have to walk the roads gathering up dead friends, listening to widows and orphans, and trying to spread hope."

Over the next three years, the archbishop became the champion of the poor and the bane of the wealthy, who sought to crush any threat to their way of life. In pastoral letters, sermons, and speeches, he described the Catholic view of justice. "The church is in the world for the benefit of mankind," he stated. "This is the meaning of service. The [Second Vatican] council puts it in theological terms: the church is a 'sign,' a 'sacrament.' . . . The church . . . understands Christ's preference for the poor, because the poor are, as [the Latin American bishops' group meeting in Colombia at] Medellin explains, those who 'place before the Latin American Church a challenge and a mission that it cannot sidestep and to which it must respond with a speed and boldness adequate to the urgency of the time.'"

This didn't mean the church wanted to become a political power, the archbishop explained. Nor was it looking for a fight. "It does not want to clash with anybody. It wants only to build up toward the great affirmation of God and his kingdom. It will clash only with those who oppose God and his kingdom. The Church wants to offer no other contribution than that of the gospel. It has no purely political contribution to make, nor any merely human skill to offer."

Quoting from the words of Pope John Paul II, he added, "When injustices increase and the gap between rich and poor widens distressingly, then the social doctrine of the Church — in a form that is creative and open to the broad areas of the Church's presence — should be a valuable tool for formation and action."

As a "logical consequence," Archbishop Romero pointed out, "of the proclamation of truth, love and the holiness of the kingdom of God, evangelization has the mission of denouncing every lie, every injustice, every sin that destroys God's plan. The purpose of this denunciation is not negative. It has a prophetic character. It seeks the conversion of those who commit the sin."

And that sin could be personal or institutional, he taught. It could be making a false god of wealth and private property, of power under the label of "national security," or even of those organizations fighting for human rights that "no longer seek the interest of the people who originally inspired them, but rather subordinate the people to the interest of ideologies and organizations."

The archbishop said, "At the base of all violence is social injustice, accurately called 'structural violence,' which is our greatest evil now." Quoting the Latin American bishops who had met at Puebla, Mexico, he continued, "This is 'the most devastating and humiliating kind of scourge,' a 'situation of inhuman poverty' finding expression in 'infant mortality, lack of adequate housing, health problems, starvation salaries, unemployment and underemployment, malnutrition, job uncertainty, [and] compulsory mass migrations.'"

And boldly he added, "Together with this structural violence, we have suffered 'repressive violence' from the state, which, justifying itself with the ideology of 'national security,' considers as 'subversive' any attempt at liberation of the people. It pretends to justify murder, disappearances, arbitrary imprisonment, acts of terrorism, kidnappings, and acts of torture,' all of which show 'a complete lack of respect for the dignity of the human person.'"

Because of all this, "the church would betray its own love for God and its fidelity to the gospel if it should cease" to be the "voice of those who do not have a voice," the "advocate of the rights of the poor," and the "counselor and promoter and humanizer of every legitimate struggle to fashion a society based on justice," one which "prepares the road to the real kingdom of God in history," Romero said.

"This demands of the church a greater closeness to the poor," but it does not relieve it of its duty to remind "the poor of their own need for conversion." The archbishop said, "The preferential option for the poor does not justify the evident moral deficiencies that the poor must correct." Being poor is not a license to sin.

And, at the same time, "the church also calls on the privileged classes—who have the responsibility of social, economic, and political power—to conversion." It "reminds them of their great responsibility in overcoming disorder and violence, not by means of repression but rather through justice and popular participation." Their "privileged situation" calls for "service to others and not paternalism," that is, not claiming that "giving what is due in justice" is really charity.

"I . . . believe," he said, "that by putting ourselves alongside the poor and trying to bring life to them we shall come to know the eternal truth of the gospel."

Through the three years Archbishop Romero headed the largest and most influential diocese in El Salvador, the violence against the poorest and those who worked with and for them continued to escalate.

In a Sunday homily on March 23, 1980, he called on the troops and members of the national guard to refuse to follow any orders to harm their fellow Salvadorans. "In the name of God, then," he said, "and in the name of this suffering people whose cries rise daily more loudly to heaven, I plead with you, I beg you, I order you in the name of God: put an end to this repression."

It soon became apparent that, in the eyes of the ruling class, he had gone too far. The next day an assassin shot and killed him while he was celebrating Mass.

"To give life to the poor one has to give of one's own life, even to give one's life itself," the archbishop had said in a speech two months before his death. "The greatest sign of faith in a God of life is the witness of those who are ready to give up their own life. 'A man can have no greater love than to lay down his life for his friends'" (John 15:13).

"Many Salvadorans, many Christians, are ready to give their lives so that the poor may have life. They are following Jesus and showing their faith in him. Living within the real world just as Jesus did, like him accused and threatened, like him laying down their lives, they are giving witness to the Word of life."

They, with Archbishop Oscar Romero among them, are the martyrs for justice.

In Scripture

It would be easier to understand what justice meant in the Bible if that concept had only one definition. It would be easier to explain it.

But Scripture scholars say justice, or righteousness, is one of those ideas that's expressed by several different words and used in many different ways. As seems to be so often the case, our single English word is a catchall that doesn't do the original text . . . justice.

In the Old Testament Hebrew, there is an implied relationship between God and his people, between God and an individual, or between two people. This means justice can refer to God, to a human, or even to a thing (the law, for example, or a way or life or even weights and measures).

Justice is at work on many levels: judicial, social, moral, and religious. But, for the Israelites, those levels overlap and are hard to distinguish because it was God who gave them the laws they follow. Scripture scholars say it's useless trying to figure out if justice originally had a legal or a religious meaning.

This doesn't mean righteousness or justice can't be seen. It can. Yahweh is righteous, of course, and always honors his promises—again going back to the covenant between God and his chosen people.

He doesn't destroy the just person with the sinner (Genesis 18:25), and he shows grace and justice (Jeremiah 9:24), especially to the oppressed (Psalm 103:6). The Israelites are righteous when they do their duty to God (Isaiah 58:2). And so is the individual (Psalm 15:2).

Justice can also be seen in God's judgment and retribution: he justly punishes the evil person (Psalm 11:6) but leads the good person to salvation. God blesses many, but that doesn't mean he lets sinners go unpunished

(Exodus 20:5). God offers both justice and grace, and those are not opposites in the Old Testament. In the Psalms, for example, they are used as parallel ideas or even identical expressions (Psalm 36:10).

The just God is ready and willing to help a person (Psalm 44:2); in that is proof of his grace (Psalm 103:6; Micah 6:5). The psalmist gives thanks for God's righteousness (51:14) when it takes the form of help in time of need (31:1).

In the Old Testament, the righteousness of God works through nature and favors the Israelites first and, among them, the religious person in particular. But, at the same time, it includes all—even animals (Psalm 36:6). God's justice lasts forever (Daniel 9:24). Because God judges all, he can make his goodness felt everywhere (Psalm 98:9).

For the religious—the righteous—person, there is absolutely no doubt that God is just (Jeremiah 12:1), but even that person can experience hard times, suffering, and martyrdom.

How does a person become righteous? God can give this virtue to a community, to an individual as a gift (Isaiah 45:8), or in the form of teaching (Hosea 10:12). It is received as salvation or as way of enabling people to act in an upright manner. Above all, the anointed of Yahweh—either the reigning king or the messianic ruler of the future—possesses God's righteousness. This allows him to rule justly and, in a special way, be the defender of, and advocate for, the poor (Psalm 72:1).

Justice is one of the essential characteristics of the messianic ruler (Jeremiah 23:5), and law and justice are in force in his kingdom (Isaiah 32:1–20). It's his duty to keep the social order that has been willed by God. In this last sense, justice isn't just a gift from God; it's also something a human achieves. To act righteously is considered an impressive accomplishment.

None of this means justice has only to do with laws. It's also a moral or religious concept warning against self-righteousness (Deuteronomy 9:4–6). The Old Testament explains that a just person is one who has the right attitude toward God and to his or her fellow human beings and lives and acts according to that. Noah is a good example (Genesis 6:9; 7:1). He was "blameless" and "walked with God." Daniel and Job were saved by their righteousness (Ezekiel 14:14, 20).

Sometimes in the Old Testament, the difference between just and unjust matches "Israelite" and "non-Israelite." The idea of the "just Israelite," or simply the "just man," can be found especially in Job, Psalms, and Proverbs. This righteousness isn't only religious or social loyalty or honesty but also faithfulness to the law for religious motives (Deuteronomy 6:25). It's the correct attitude in applying the law (Leviticus

19:15) and behavior based on upright social principles (Exodus 23:6). Here, tying in with another virtue, justice is also applying practical wisdom (Proverbs 2:1, 9). So giving money to the poor and performing good works are also acts of righteousness that can atone for sin and bring salvation (Daniel 4:27).

In the New Testament, righteousness (or, again, justice) refers to the moral-religious goodness of a person. Luke 1:6 describes it as "living blamelessly according to all the commandments and regulations of the Lord." It is being blameless.

"The way of righteousness" (Matthew 21:32) means a life that's lived according to God's commandments. To be just is to follow Yahweh's law. And certainly the prime example of someone who lived that way, who followed the law, is Jesus (Matthew 13:17). In the Beatitudes, delivered as part of his Sermon on the Mount, he promises God will fill—will satisfy—those who "hunger and thirst for righteousness" (Matthew 5:6).

This righteousness that is demanded by Christ is greater and more perfect than that exhibited by the scribes and Pharisees (Matthew 5:20). It emphasizes the intention of the law rather than legalistic observance (Matthew 6:1), what we today would call following the spirit of the law and not simply its letter. Jesus stresses this in Matthew 5:21–48.

For the New Testament writers, justice is essentially a gift from God. This means he's the one who makes it happen. A part of God's kingdom, justice has as its source God's grace.

In Paul's writing, "righteousness of God" is tied in with grace, salvation, justification, and faith. Christ is our "righteousness" (1 Corinthians 1:30), and we have become "the righteousness of God" (2 Corinthians 5:21). The only way to share in righteousness is faith in Jesus, which means an individual needs to totally accept the saving revelation of God in Christ.

For Paul, faith and grace are intimately and inseparably joined, and either can be referred to as the basis of righteousness (Romans 3:22; Galatians 5:4). Through faith and through grace, we can become people of justice.

Down through the Ages

"Because the world is forgetting God, . . . injustice to neighbor and inhumanity to the weak prevail," St. Basil the Great wrote in the fourth century.

Basil (ca. 329–79), the bishop of Caesarea in Asia Minor, came from a family that produced a number of saints over three generations, including two of his brothers and a sister. A Father and Doctor of the church, he's remembered for his books that refuted the Arian heresy (which said Jesus was not divine), a treatise on the Holy Spirit, many homilies, and several rules on monastic life. He's called the Father of Monasticism in the East.

In a work titled *On Mercy and Justice*, the bishop presented the unbreakable bond between those two virtues. "The law contains many injunctions forbidding us to wrong our neighbor and many precepts directing us to be merciful and compassionate," he wrote. "If either of these admonitions be neglected, the other does not by itself justify a man. Benefactions to the needy, financed by unjust gains, are not acceptable with God; yet, a man who refrains from committing injustices, but does not share the goods he possesses with anyone, is not deserving of praise."

In other words, if a person makes a fortune by taking advantage of others and then donates part of her money to help others, she isn't acting justly. And if another person earns a living without acting unjustly but refuses to share his resources with anyone, he isn't any better than the first person.

"You must, therefore, combine justice with mercy," Basil wrote, "spending in mercy what you possess with justice, as it is written 'Keep mercy and justice and draw near to God always'" (Hosea 12:6). Because God loves mercy and justice, he continued, the person who takes care to do both "draws near to him."

That's why each of us must examine our actions, and "the rich man [needs] to take careful inventory of the private resources from which he is to offer gifts to God, to make sure that he has not oppressed a poor man, or used force against one weaker than himself, or cheated one dependent on him, thus exercising license rather than justice." (It's not hard to take that warning and apply it not just personally but socially or nationally. True "humanitarian" aid can't have any form of exploitation as its funding source.)

In a teaching that sounds grossly out of place in our own time but that reflects the age in which Basil lived, the bishop added, "We are bidden to practice fairness and justice also toward our slaves." More in sync with our society, he continued, "Do not employ force because you are in command and do not take advantage because it is within your power to do so." No, "on the contrary, show forth the deeds of justice because you are able to perform the deeds of power."

What if we do make a mistake? What if we do commit the sin of injustice? Then "be merciful to the one whom you have wronged. Exercise benevolence toward him. Show him kindness and you will fulfill the duty of mercy with justice." Know that "God will have no part of avarice nor will the Lord be a comrade to thieves and robbers." And remember that God "has not left us the poor to feed because he is unable to do this, but he asks from us, for our own good, the fruit of justice and mercy." He give us the opportunity to be just and merciful.

But "to the man who refrains from committing injustice, but is negligent in showing mercy, we say: 'every tree that does not yield fruit shall be cut down and cast into the fire' [Matthew 3:10]. Never will such a tree be pleasing to the divine Husbandman." However, those who, "by showing mercy, sharing their goods, and conferring benefits . . . may produce in themselves the benevolence of God. 'Give,' he says, 'and it will be given to you.'"

The bishop remarked, "Furthermore, he has promised that if they produce these virtues, they will be united with him. . . . He who ministers zealously to the poor man becomes a comrade of Christ—not only if he be rich and share great possessions, but even if he offers to the needy the little he has."

This is true because the needs of others, which the world sees as "poverty, is a source of true riches to you" because, by helping answer that need with mercy and justice, "you become thereby a co-worker with Christ."

St. Margaret of Scotland (d. 1093) never wrote about justice. None of her words can be quoted here. But one of her contemporaries, a priest named Turgot who was her confessor, wrote of her. His description shows she understood how to live this virtue in her own life and how to promote it. Her actions, and her legacy, describe justice.

A member of the highest English and continental royalty, Margaret was brought up in a religious setting by Benedictines in Hungary. Under their tutelage, she became familiar with the works of John Cassian and Gregory the Great as well as Augustine. She was sent to England in her early teens and then to Scotland, where she captivated King Malcolm of Canmore. She was twenty-four when they married.

As queen of Scotland, Margaret followed three tracks: personal piety that included asceticism; reformation of the church in Scotland (which, because of its distance from Rome, had developed some of its own, at times misguided, traditions); and justice to everyone within her realm, from slaves to royalty. She was successful at all of them.

"She thought it beneath her dignity to fix her affection upon the things of the world," Turgot wrote, "so that good works delighted her more than riches. By means of her temporal possessions she earned for herself the rewards of Heaven; for there, where her heart was, she had placed her treasure also. And since before all things she sought the kingdom of God and his justice, the bountiful grace of the Almighty freely added to her honors and riches in abundance. . . . Nothing was firmer than her fidelity, steadier than her favor, or juster than her decisions; nothing more enduring than her patience, graver than her advice or more pleasant than her conversation."

Her biographer noted she never fully "tamed" King Malcolm, but "by the help of God she made him most attentive to the works of justice, mercy, almsgiving and other virtues." Malcolm couldn't read, but he realized the books to which she often referred, including those of the Fathers of the Church, were among the sources of her great wisdom. She pointed out the injustices within his realm, and he backed her up when she called for changes.

At the same time, Margaret took a hands-on approach to helping the poor and sick, and she insisted her children, six boys and two girls, do likewise. Among her rules for her family were "to be charitable to the poor, to protect orphans and relieve them in their necessities."

As Turgot explained, "She took all heed that they should be well brought up and especially that they should be trained in virtue."

Margaret died at the age of forty-seven, just days after her husband and a son had been killed in battle. One daughter later married Henry I of England and became known as "Good Queen Maud." Three sons — Edgar,

Alexander, and David—successively became king of Scotland. David was canonized a saint.

Their mother had shown them, by word and deed, the heart of justice.

In our own time, Anglican archbishop Desmond Tutu of South Africa often spoke out on and wrote about justice. The Nobel Peace Prize winner was a strong opponent of the apartheid system that governed his homeland for decades. His criticism of those in authority placed his own safety in jeopardy.

In an address given in Pretoria while the struggle continued, Tutu said the church "must be there in the poverty and squalor"—that is, the result of injustice—"to bring the love and compassion of God amongst the sick, the hungry, the lepers, the disabled and the naked." Its members must "proclaim . . . in a country of injustice and oppression . . . that this is God's world."

The archbishop said, "He [God] is on the side of the oppressed, of the poor, of the despised ones. We must say these things even if they make us suffer. It is not politics. It is the Gospel of Jesus Christ the liberator who will set us free."

But to demand justice in this way, to identify with the poor, "is a costly business," he continued. "It leads to vilification and ostracism. Christ not only suffered but was eventually killed for it. If the Church is a serving Church, it will be a suffering Church as well. . . . An affluent, comfortable Church cannot be the Church of Christ—an affluent Church which uses its wealth for itself."

No, the church—meaning, also, those who are its members—has to be "the salt and light of the world." We are "the hope of the hopeless, through the power of God." As such, we're called upon to "transfigure a situation of hate and suspicion, of brokenness and separation, of fear and bitterness." We have no choice because "we are servants of the God who reigns and cares."

God "wants us to be an alternative society," the one in which justice and mercy prevail. "Where there is harshness and insensitivity, we must be compassionate and caring; where people are statistics, we must show they count as being of immense value to God; where there is grasping and selfishness, we must be a sharing community now."

Tutu reminded his listeners that people were attracted to the early church "not so much by the preaching, but by the fact that they saw Christians as a community, living a new life as if what God had done was important, and had made a difference." It was a community of "those who, whether poor or rich, male or female, free or slave, young or old— all quite unbelievably loved and cared for each other." It was their lifestyle that showed others outside the church what it meant to follow Christ.

And, in another address, the Nobel laureate described how Christ himself was one who lived a just life: "Nowhere are we told that he ever turned anybody away who was in need; no matter how busy he was he never neglected anybody. . . . He sat at the table with all the riff-raff of the town, those whom every respectable person would not be seen dead with, let alone supping with them—those prostitutes, those sinners, those drug addicts, the so-called scum of society."

Jesus "revolutionized religion by showing that God was really a disreputable God, a God on the side of social pariahs. He showed God as one who accepted sinners unconditionally."

And, Tutu stressed, "he was a man of prayer, a man of God. . . . Prayer and spirituality were central in the life of our Lord, and he was the man for others only because first and foremost he had been the man of God."

For Us Today

There's never been a child who hasn't screamed, "That's not fair!" There's never been a parent who hasn't answered, "Life's not fair."

It isn't. Someone gets a bigger piece of cake. Someone gets to stay up later at night. Someone doesn't have as much homework.

Someone gets a newer car. Someone gets a promotion. Someone seems to live a charmed life, skating through the years worry free.

Eventually, we all learn, usually the hard way, that life on earth is not fair and never will be. What we then mistakenly presume is there's nothing we can do about it. But justice says we can do something; it says we must. And we must do something prudently and temperately because the virtue of justice doesn't have merely an opposite vice (injustice), but a host of pitfalls if carried to an extreme.

The first is the messiah complex. If we love justice, if we fight for those who are oppressed in some way, we can come to see ourselves as the great savior. There's no room for charity as we crush those who, it seems to us, are promoting injustice. We use any means necessary, justifying our actions by saying the end will be good. We scoff at, badger, and denounce those who don't fight the same battle as diligently as we do, whatever that particular battle might be. We come to believe our solutions to the problem are so astute, so brilliant, so holy, we don't even need to cloud the issue by listening to what those who are oppressed have to say. We know best. They just have to trust us.

The second is the sin of self-righteousness. We have every reason, every right, to be as critical as we want because we are steeped in the facts and figures of our cause. We know the Truth—with a capital *T*—and any other opinion, argument, or proposed solution is pure poppy-cock. God and we, not necessarily in that order, have deemed our way is *the* way. Case closed.

The third is the fault of judgmental behavior. We divide the world into the pure and the tainted, and, as far as we can see, we are the only ones truly spotless. We look down on those whom we judge less virtuous than ourselves. We don't hesitate to throw a spotlight on their failings or announce that punishment, temporal or eternal, awaits them. Our harsh ruling allows no room for mercy.

And the fourth is one that might be called "loving globally but being a real stinker locally." We always join the latest international cause—putting the sticker on our car's bumper, writing the check to the humanitarian organization, going on and on about the issues to anyone polite enough to listen—but we treat the folks around us like dirt. We have no time, patience, energy, or sympathy for the people with whom we come into contact daily.

Justice is a difficult virtue. Not simply because it's hard to live justly, which it is, but because it's hard to know *how* to live justly. Where do we begin? In our hearts. In our homes. Where will it lead us? Only God knows. What we can be certain of is that, at some point, in some way, it will bring us to the cross. To live justly is to walk toward Calvary. There are no exceptions. Justice is going to cost us.

How to begin? We need to listen. The Lord hears the cries of the poor (Job 34:28). We can't become so caught up in our own life or our own worries, no matter how serious our problems may be, that we shut out all others. We can't allow ourselves to become so over-whelmed by the sights and the sounds (again, the glitter and splash) of what the world offers that we're blind and deaf to the needs, to the rights, of the poor.

Jesus has told us that when they cry, he cries. When they hunger, he hungers. When they are lonely, he is lonely. Justice leads us to them, and in doing so it leads us to him. Small wonder, then, that so many who serve others give the same response: "I get so much more out of it than I give." Jesus said when we serve them, we serve him. This isn't news to us. We've all heard it before. But hearing it, truly believing it, and then consistently acting on that belief are three very different things.

It's tempting to limit the virtue of justice to fighting for workers' rights or decent housing or access to proper medical care. Certainly that's a part of justice. But it's broader than that. Fortunately, parts of it are simpler. Closer

to home. Justice can be comforting someone
who is grieving. Feeding someone who is hungry. Being with someone who is lonely. It can
be immediate and concrete. It can be uncom-
plicated and obvious.

In recent times, this aspect of justice, so
closely tied to charity, has come under criticism. "It's slapping a bandage on the problem,"
the argument goes, "rather than treating its
source and causes. No, justice is dealing with
the issue in a larger way. Give a person a fish
and he eats for a day; teach a person to fish and
he's fed for a lifetime."

That point of view has merit because it's
true. But, at the same time, it's misleading
because it isn't the complete truth. Sometimes
we need that bandage right now, even as the
larger cause and problem begin to be
addressed. Sometimes we need that fish right
now, even as we learn how to fish.

Justice isn't either/or. It's both/and. St.
Paul tells us there are many gifts but the same
Spirit (1 Corinthians 12:4). In justice, some of
us are called to focus on ministering here and
now. In justice, some of us are called to address
the bigger picture. Neither is the wrong way to
practice this virtue. And neither alone is *the*
right way.

If we take the time, if we make the effort to
listen for the cries of the poor, we will also hear

God calling us to respond in the way that is correct for us. For some of us, at this point in our lives, it may be limited to praying for those in need. Others may establish a one-on-one relationship (or reestablish a relationship) in the family, at work, or in the community that has suffered damage. Some of us may be able to contribute money to the organizations that promote Christian justice. Others might discover their vocation and career is service to others. Some may set aside time to volunteer. Others may realize they are being called to shift jobs or, if retired, begin a second career that centers on justice.

How do we know what's right for us? The more we become a person of prayer, a person of God, the more we will discover not just where society or our own immediate world is unjust and needs correction but where we ourselves suffer from that fault and need to change. We'll learn that the more we work on removing the beam from our own eye, the greater our ability to help another remove the speck from his or hers.

And always, always, we need to remember the relationship between justice and mercy because God extends both to us. His justice is cradled in mercy. Christian justice is not strident, is not vindictive, is not the Old Testament's eye for an eye (Exodus 21:24). (So many of us remember that single passage so clearly when we want to get even while ignoring the words in Matthew 18:22 of forgiveness and compassion that replaced it, calling on us to forgive one another seventy-seven times — meaning always.)

Scripture tells us God loves justice (Psalm 33:5). Why? Because he is just, and when we practice this virtue, we are not merely imitating him, we are living in the manner for which we were created. He made us to be just. To practice the virtue of justice is to become more like God, even as we continue to find our way home to him by serving others, which is serving him.

To Read More about It

Gerard Beigel, *Faith and Social Justice in the Teaching of John Paul II* (New York: Peter Lang, 1997).

Bill Dodds and Michael J. Dodds, O.P., *Living the Beatitudes Today: Happily Ever After Begins Here and Now* (Chicago: Loyola Press, 1997).

Oscar Romero, *Voice of the Voiceless* (Maryknoll, N.Y.: Orbis Books, 1990).

Desmond Tutu, *The Rainbow People of God* (New York: Doubleday, 1994).

Fortitude

In One Life

When Raymond Kolbe was ten years old, he had a vision that shaped his life and his death.

Born in 1894 in a town near Lodz, Poland, young Kolbe was what we might call a handful. Not malicious, just busy. The story is told that one day his mother, half-joking, half-serious, asked him, "What is going to become of you?"

He took her question seriously and considered it for several days. It was after that, while stopping by the parish church to say a prayer, that Raymond saw Mary. She appeared to him holding two crowns: a white one indicating purity and a gold one (or, some biographers say, a red one) for martyrdom. The choice was his. He brashly told her he wanted both.

After that, Raymond became more serious and more obedient. He entered the Franciscan Conventuals in 1907, taking the name Maximilian. Highly intelligent, he was sent to study in Rome in 1912, eventually earning doctorates in philosophy and theology. He was ordained there in 1918.

Devotion to Mary had always been a central part of his spirituality. He believed the route to personal holiness was consecrating oneself to God through Mary. A year before his ordination, he began a movement based on that principle. Members of his Militia Immaculata (or Militia of Mary Immaculate) devoted themselves to worldwide evangelization by dedicating themselves to Christ through Mary.

In 1919, Father Maximilian returned to Poland and began teaching in Kraków. He also started forming small Militia Immaculata prayer groups. Three years later, he received permission to begin publishing a magazine called *Knight of Mary Immaculate*, but only on the condition that he raise all the money for it himself. His order would not be able to help finance it.

The publication was a huge hit. At one point, circulation topped one million. Building on that success, in 1927 Father Maximilian was able to begin what he called the "City of Mary Immaculate," a center dedicated to Marian devotion. Despite poor health, including tuberculosis and only partial use of one lung, the young priest had founded the largest Catholic publishing house in Poland and the largest Franciscan friary in the world, with some seven hundred friars and brothers living there.

Three years later, in 1930, he left Poland with four fellow Franciscans and traveled to Nagasaki, Japan. He began publishing a magazine there and established a friary before returning to his homeland six years later.

After Poland fell to the Nazis in September 1939, *Knight of Mary Immaculate* magazine was forbidden, and eventually Father Maximilian was arrested. He was considered an enemy agitator, known for having published articles that were critical of the Third Reich. He was released but was arrested once again in February 1941.

During the time between his two arrests, the Nazis kept a close eye on him and on the City of Mary Immaculate. One friar recalled, "In those grave and unpleasant meetings, Father Maximilian spoke with sober dignity. His behavior toward the Gestapo agents was always completely serene—he had absolutely no fear of them—but prudent."

A brother noted, "In spite of all this—the dispersion [friars sent to various places], imprisonment, numerous oppressions, and deprivations, including even the requisitioning of our food—Father Maximilian not only never showed even anger, let alone hate for the Germans, but kept exhorting us friars to pray for their conversion and to *love* them."

He also kept applying for permission to resume publishing *Knight of Mary Immaculate* but understood what he and his friars faced. "Now after our transaction with the German authorities," he said after his first arrest, "if they take us to their camp or take our lives, ours will be a martyr's death for the faith."

It was while in prison the first time that Father Maximilian was repeatedly and harshly slapped in the face for wearing his habit, which included a rosary. With each blow, the guard pointed to the crucifix and asked if the priest believed in what or who it represented. And each time Father Maximilian said he did. "He struck Father Kolbe in the face again and again," an eyewitness, a fellow prisoner, would later recall. "But, finally, seeing that Father Kolbe could not be shaken, he gave up and stomped angrily from the cell, slamming the door." Throughout the ordeal, "Father Kolbe showed not the slightest agitation." And afterwards, it was the priest who comforted the eyewitness, who was greatly disturbed by what he had seen.

When Father Maximilian was rearrested in early 1941, he blessed his fellow Franciscans as

he was led away. He told them they would not
be seeing him again.

After spending time in the local prison,
Father Maximilian was sent by boxcar to
Auschwitz, where the Nazis had a particular
hatred for priests. "To some extent," one biographer explained, "priests and Jews were
lumped together in the SS mind."

"We were in constant terror," a priest said
later. "It was like a psychosis. What were they
doing this to us for? We could not even trust
one another because sometimes there were
spies among the prisoners. Religious practices
were forbidden. Even prayer was not allowed
on pain of severe beating or being put to death.
We priests still got together occasionally to
pray in common, but no one dared single himself out to deliver a sermon, which could have
marked him for death. The exception, of
course, after his arrival was Father Kolbe, who
said he was willing to put his life on the line to
bring others to Christ."

Father Kolbe was assigned the most brutal
manual labor. Pausing for any reason brought
an immediate beating (or sometimes a prisoner
was simply killed on the spot). The Franciscan
had suffered his share of blows when one day
a guard singled him out for special attention.
He was forced to try to carry an extremely
heavy load of branches, and when he failed, he

was kicked time and again in the face and stomach. Then the head guard ordered him to lie across a stump, and he summoned other guards known for their strength. They gave Father Kolbe fifty lashes.

When they had finished, Father Kolbe couldn't move. When it was time to march back from the workstation to the barracks, other prisoners had to carry him. The next day, he was taken to the camp hospital. Besides suffering injuries from the beating, he had a high fever because of pneumonia and, probably, typhus.

In time, he was given a lower bunk by the door. Each dead man who was carried out received his blessing. He told stories to the other patients to lift their spirits, led prayers, and gave conferences on Mary Immaculate. After dark, prisoners crawled to his bedside to go to confession and seek comfort. Having been famous throughout Poland before the war, he now became known among the prisoners as "our little father."

"His words . . . were simple and profound," said one man who had crawled to him. "He urged me to have firm faith in the victory of good. 'Hate is not creative; only love is creative,' he whispered, pressing my hand warmly in his ardor. 'These sufferings will not cause us to crumble but will help us more and more to become stronger.'"

After being released from the hospital, Father Kolbe cleaned latrines, shoveled manure, and peeled potatoes.

"I owe to him that I am still alive," another prisoner has stated, "that I was able to hold out and lived to be liberated." In a world filled with violence, starvation, and disease, "I began to feel why not end it all by throwing myself on the wire [of the electric fences] the way other prisoners did." One day, he rushed toward the fence but was grabbed, made to go back, and beaten.

Father Kolbe heard about what had happened. "He talked to me and calmed me down," the man said. "The things he said had such an effect on me that I never thought of committing suicide again. Not only brave himself, he communicated that bravery to me and to others I could name. . . .

"I recall his saying, 'I don't fear death; I fear sin.' He kept encouraging us not to be afraid of dying, but to have at heart the salvation of our souls. He said that if we feared nothing but sin, prayed to Christ and sought the intercession of Mary, we would know peace. He pointed Christ out to us as the one sure support and help we could count on."

Through June and July 1941, Father Kolbe "courageously gathered us secretly together almost every day . . . to instruct us. . . . He assured us that, although not all would survive, all of us would conquer." Father Kolbe's greatest act of courage, his greatest act of faith, is well documented. His fellow prisoners remembered well the day he stepped forward from the ranks.

A man was missing from Father Kolbe's barracks, and it was presumed he was trying to escape. In retribution, 10 men were to be chosen at random from the remaining 599 and sent to die in the starvation bunker. When one of the condemned began to cry out about his wife and children, Father Kolbe stepped forward and volunteered to take his place.

Eyewitnesses consider it a miracle that the priest wasn't shot for simply stepping out of the ranks. That he wasn't beaten or had the dogs set on him. That the deputy commander didn't just add Father Kolbe to the group. But none of those things happened. Instead, Father Kolbe was allowed to take the other man's place. (The one he saved, Francis Gajowniczek, survived the war and went on to tell, time and again, of the Franciscan's courage.)

For two weeks, Father Kolbe encouraged his fellow prisoners in their tiny, dark cell. Another prisoner who acted as an interpreter for the guards recalled that time: "What kind of martyrdom these men were enduring can be imagined from the fact that the urine bucket was always dry. In their dreadful thirst, they must have drunk its contents."

One by one, the men died. When only four were left, the Nazis decided it was taking too long. They entered the cell and injected carbolic acid in each of them, including Father Kolbe, who was still conscious. Death came in a matter of seconds. The bodies of all the dead were taken to the crematorium.

"To say that Father Kolbe died for one of us or for that person's family is too great a simplification," a prisoner later said. "His death was the salvation of thousands." He gave those he met, and those who learned of his sacrifice, a new optimism, a new strength, a new courage.

"We were stunned by his act," the man explained, "which became for us a mighty explosion of light in the dark camp night."

In Scripture

Adam and Eve had no fortitude, no courage. Mary did.

The story of our first parents in the book of Genesis is the tale of their disobeying God, damaging the relationship they had with him, and then being fearful of the consequence. They hide until the Lord comes looking for them.

Adam finally confesses, "I heard the sound of you in the garden, and I was afraid, because I was naked; and I hid myself" (Genesis 3:10).

Mary's story is the opposite. She has done nothing wrong when an angel appears to her. She's "much perplexed"—there's an understatement—and so the angel assures her, "Do not be afraid" (Luke 1:29–30). By God's gracious will, she has been chosen to be mother of the Messiah. No matter how frightening all this might seem, no matter how impossible, her response is, "Let it be with me according to your word" (1:38).

Any religious fear or fearlessness in Scripture lies between these two extremes.

Throughout the Old Testament, God asks those who are dear to him to put aside their fears. "The word of the Lord came to Abram in a vision, 'Do not be afraid, Abram, I am your shield'" (Genesis 15:1). "And that very night the Lord appeared to him [Isaac] and said, 'I am the God of your father Abraham; do not be afraid, for I am with you'" (Genesis 26:24). "Know that I [the Lord] am with you [Jacob] and will keep you wherever you go" (Genesis 28:15).

When God makes himself known to an individual or shows his powers to a crowd, there is fear. Take Moses on Mount Sinai, for example: "When all the people witnessed the thunder and lightning, the sound of the trumpet, and the mountain smoking, they were afraid and trembled and stood at a distance" (Exodus 20:18).

On the other hand, because they are God's chosen people, the Israelites don't have to be afraid of their enemies. "Have no dread or fear of them," Moses says. "The Lord your God, who goes before you, is the one who will fight for you, just as he did for you in Egypt before your very eyes, and in the wilderness, where you saw how the Lord your God carried you, just as one carries a child, all the way that you traveled until you reached this place" (Deuteronomy 1:29–31).

Then he adds, "But in spite of this, you have no trust in the Lord your God, who goes before you on the way to seek out a place for you to camp, in fire by night, and in the cloud by day, to show you the route you should take" (1:32).

"Fear of the Lord" meant just that. Being afraid of God and his power. It was the great motivation to obey his laws. Over time, the original meaning developed into the idea of showing proper religious awe for the Creator. This is how the term is used in the Psalms. "You who fear the Lord, praise him!" (22:23). To fear God is to be pious. "Those who fear the Lord will have a happy end; on the day of their death they will be blessed" (Sirach 1:13).

At that same time, the Old Testament records acts by individuals, male and female, that would be considered courageous and even gruesome by any people of any time. Among the women: Deborah leads troops into war, and Jael kills the enemy's leader by driving a tent peg into his temple (Judges 4–5). Later, Judith helps save the Israelites by hacking off the head of another enemy leader (Judith 13:6–10).

In the New Testament, people are sometimes afraid when they watch Jesus perform miracles, such as the raising of the widow's son from the dead. "Fear seized all of them; and they glorified God, saying, 'A great prophet has risen among us!'" (Luke 7:16). Even among his disciples, there is also a sense of awe at his power. At the Transfiguration, "they fell to the ground and were overcome by fear" (Matthew 17:6).

Christ continues to tell them they do not have to be afraid, even though they may face persecution and death. Their heavenly Father will not fail to take care of his "little flock" (Luke 12:32). Even when almost all of them abandon Jesus on Calvary, when their lack of courage sends them scurrying for hiding places, they are not condemned because of their fear. After his resurrection, Christ returns in their midst (scaring them once more), but the words he has told them earlier hit home: "Take courage; I have conquered the world!" (John 16:33).

On Pentecost, the Holy Spirit gives the apostles a boldness that, it seems safe to speculate, before then was unimaginable to them. The same is offered to all Christians. "For you did not receive a spirit of slavery to fall back into fear," Paul writes to the community in Rome, "but you have received a spirit of adoption. When we cry, 'Abba! Father!' it is that very Spirit bearing witness with our spirit that we are children of God, and if children, then heirs, heirs of God and joint heirs with Christ — if, in fact, we suffer with him so that we may also be gloried with him" (Romans 8:15).

But, at the same time, Christians can't get cocky because each must work out his or her "own salvation with fear and trembling" (Philippians 2:12). It is God who inspires fear, just as he did in the early Old Testament, and it is God who takes it away.

None of this means the devout Christian is never afraid. Paul writes of his own "weakness," "fear," and "much trembling" (1 Corinthians 2:3). The first letter credited to Peter stresses that Jesus' followers are to fear God (1 Peter 2:17) and act accordingly as long as they are on earth (1 Peter 1:17).

John points out how love removes fear. "There is no fear in love, but perfect love casts out fear; for fear has to do with punishment, and whoever fears has not reached perfection in love" (1 John 4:18). Those who have united themselves completely to God have no reason to be afraid. And while we won't reach that level of love here on earth, we can continue to move toward it.

Down through the Ages

It's easy to romanticize the martyrdom the early Christians faced. But pain then was as real as it is today. In the third century, St. Cyprian (d. 258) wrote about that pain and about the courage it took to face it.

Born a pagan, Cyprian studied law and was a teacher and rhetorician (a public speaker) before joining the church around 246. Two years later, he was elected bishop of Carthage (in northern Africa), and the following year, he had to flee when a new round of persecutions began. Cyprian kept in contact with his people by writing to them frequently. His letters give a picture of the times and the challenges the followers of Christ were facing then.

After he was able to return to Carthage in 251, he played a key role in sorting out how to deal with "lapsed" Christians who wanted to return to the church. These were people who had, in one way or another, denied their faith during persecution to avoid punishment, including death. Theologians weren't in agreement, and at times Cyprian and the pope were at odds.

Between 252 and 254, Carthage faced a terrible plague. Cyprian organized the Christians there and strongly told them they had a duty to care not only for their fellow believers but also for their enemies and persecutors. In 257, Cyprian was ordered to worship Roman gods. When he refused, he was exiled and, a year later after continuing to refuse, was beheaded.

"With what praises can I commend you, most courageous brothers?" Cyprian had written to others who had faced what was to become his fate. "With what vocal proclamation can I extol the strength of your heart and the perseverance of your faith? You have borne the sharpest examination by torture, even unto the glorious consummation, and have not yielded to suffering, but rather the sufferings have given way to you."

He continued, "The multitude of those who were present saw with admiration the heavenly contest—the contest of God, the spiritual contest, the battle of Christ—saw that his servants stood with free voice, with unyielding mind, with divine virtue, bare, indeed, of weapons of this world, but believing and armed with the weapons of faith. . . . The tortured stood more brave than the torturers. . . . The scourge, often repeated with all its rage, could not conquer invincible faith."

Cyprian had encouragement, too, for those who were going to face brutal and barbaric punishment. "If the battle shall call you out, if the day of your contest shall come, engage bravely, fight with constancy . . . knowing that you are fighting under the eyes of a present Lord, that you are attaining by the confession of his name to his own glory."

He wrote, "The struggle is one [meaning it's always the same conflict], but it is crowded with a multitude of contests." (Persecution brings a variety of hardships and challenges.) "You conquer hunger, and despise thirst, and tread under foot the squalor of the dungeon, and the horror of the very abode of punishment, by the vigor of your courage. Punishment is there subdued; torture worn out; death is not feared but desired, being overcome by the reward of immortality, so that he who has conquered is crowned with eternity of life."

Cyprian also noted, "We are not . . . to yield because they threaten; nor is the adversary and enemy on that account greater than Christ, because he claims for himself so much in the world. There ought to abide in us, dearest brother, an immovable strength of faith; and against all the eruptions and onsets of the waves that roar against us, a steady and unshaken courage should plant itself as with the fortitude and mass of a resisting rock."

More than a millennium later, long after Christianity was no longer outlawed, a Catholic teenage girl came along who personified that ancient virtue fortitude. In religious art, the Old Testament's Judith had been the exemplar of courage, but in nonreligious art, fortitude was simply a woman in armor.

St. Joan of Arc became that woman. Not only did she dress that way (at a time when it was extremely rare for females to do so), but her courageous action both in battle and after being captured and condemned to death showed her to be the epitome of bravery. French-English politics aside, the story of Joan of Arc is the tale of one girl's unshakable faith in God. Born in 1412, she left home to aid her country in 1429. Four months later, at Orléans, she fought her first battle. The next year, she was captured and the following year, at the age of nineteen, burned at the stake as a witch and sorceress. A victim of war, unjustly slain for heresy, Joan was not forgotten. Her courage was recalled but so, too, was her piety. Though illiterate, she had spoken to those in authority with assurance about the visions she had seen and voices she had heard that prodded her into action.

Writing about her last moments, a witness would recall that "beside her walked Friar Martin and myself, with an escort of eight hundred soldiers armed with axes and swords.

And when she came to the Vieux Marché she listened to the sermon with great fortitude and most calmly, showing signs and evidence and clear proof of her contrition, penitence, and fervent faith. . . . Also she most humbly begged all manner of people, of whatever condition or rank they might be, and whether of her party or of the other, for their pardon, and asked them to kindly pray for her, at the same time pardoning them any harm they had done her."

Joan had earlier testified that, starting at the age of thirteen, it had been St. Michael the Archangel (the great warrior angel), St. Margaret of Antioch (an early martyr), and St. Catherine of Alexandria (the patroness of maidens) whom she had seen and heard.

Another Catherine, of Siena, had yet to be canonized during Joan's time. But this Doctor of the Church (ca.1347–80), Dominican, mystic, and author had written of fortitude in her *The Dialogue:* "If you will observe the virtues of fortitude and perseverance, these virtues are proved by the long endurance of the injuries and detractions of wicked men, who, whether by injuries or by flattery, constantly endeavor to turn a man aside from following the road and the doctrine of truth. Wherefore, in all these things, the virtue of fortitude conceived within the soul, perseveres with strength, and, in addition, proves itself externally upon the neighbor. . . . And if fortitude were not able to make that good proof of itself, being tested by many contrarities, it would not be a serious virtue founded in truth."

The world, at times, offers both the carrot and the stick. Fortitude allows the Christian to remain faithful in spite of either temptation, showing others what having strength in Jesus (and through him) really means.

Yet another Catherine, this one in the twentieth century, described how that strength, that faith, can overcome the fears the modern world brings. She, too, is an example of Christian fortitude.

Catherine de Hueck Doherty was born into a wealthy Russian family in 1896 and married when she was fifteen. The couple was forced to flee Communist Russia in 1920 and settled, penniless, in Canada. There they had a son and eventually were financially successful again. But Catherine's husband was abusive and unfaithful, so she left him. (Later they divorced, and the marriage was annulled by the church.)

Haunted by Christ's words "Sell all that you have and give to the poor, and come, follow me," Catherine sold her possessions in 1930, keeping only enough to provide for her child, and then mother and son went to live with the poor in the slums of Toronto in a

"Friendship House." In 1938, she was invited to work in Harlem in an interracial apostolate. Five years later, she married Eddie Doherty, a well-known newspaper reporter; in 1947, they founded Madonna House, a rural settlement in Combermere, Ontario. It became a training center for the lay apostolate.

Catherine died there in 1985. (Eddie, who eventually was ordained a priest in the Melkite Rite, had passed away ten years earlier.) Since then, Madonna House has grown to more than two hundred members, with twenty-three "field houses" throughout the world. More than 125 priests, deacons, and bishops are associates.

In her best-known work, *Poustinia: Christian Spirituality of the East for Western Man,* Catherine described the relationship between faith and fear. (*Poustinia,* the first syllable of which is pronounced like the English word *pew,* is Russian for "desert." "In the Western sense of the word," Catherine explained, "it would mean a place to which a hermit goes, and, hence, it could be called a hermitage.")

"If we have faith in God, we must have faith in men," she wrote. "Even the most evil among us has some redeeming feature. Faith will seek it out.

"It is so important for us to have faith, trust, confidence in one another. It is the only way we can communicate. Without faith there is no communication, there is no love, or if there was a little love it will die without hope, trust, and confidence. Even if it doesn't die right away, it will be so ill, so weak, and so tired that communication will be miserable as well.

"Faith alone can restore communication. Yes, it is time we should believe in one another. It is time we should return to God and ask to be healed from this strange lack of faith, this strange lack of confidence and trust in one another. This is the moment, this is the hour to turn our face to God and ask to be healed from the fear of trusting, from the fear of confiding, from the fear of believing in one another."

She continued, "Let faith, hope, love, trust, and confidence reign among us. Let us be done with human respect. Let us be done with being afraid of ridicule. Let us be done with thinking we have to hide anything from one another."

In another section, describing a self-examination of her own life and attitude, she noted, "If I were really given over to the will of God totally, then I would fear nothing, and I would be totally free. I wouldn't need any defenses, any weapons, any psychological coping devices. What for? In everything that happened to me, I would say: 'Such is God's pleasure.' I would accept whatever comes to me with joy."

She recalled, "My thoughts turned to death at this moment. Man fundamentally fears death above everything else. He fears dissolution. But with this defenselessness that leads to total freedom, there would be no fear, no defenses against even death. And I looked back upon my life. True, the Lord put me through a little novitiate of defenselessness. For I have been persecuted. I have been ill. I have lived in great poverty for quite a while. Looking back, I saw that I was defenseless, or tried to be. I also saw that I failed sometimes, and put up little defenses against people who tried to persecute me.

"But now I understood that God wanted me to give up even these defenses—all of them. Defenselessness against death, defenselessness against people, defenselessness against everything—for defenselessness was holy. It gave you total freedom. The soul then would truly walk in the footsteps of Christ who was led like a lamb to the slaughter and accepted it all, including death. Then the person would experience resurrection right here and now.

"He would have the freedom of the children of God. He would really know that God has ceased to call him a servant and now calls him His friend!"

For Us Today

We need fortitude because so much of life is unknown, and the unknown is frightening.

We need fortitude because to follow Christ is to clash with what the world believes and teaches and insists. It's so easy, so tempting, to be swept away by it.

We need fortitude because we are imperfect. We fall and are asked to rise again.

We need fortitude because one day we will die.

It's easy to make the mistake of believing that this virtue has to do with eliminating fear. But that's not true. Fortitude, or courage, isn't the absence of fear. Many a brave person has admitted he or she remained frightened while committing some heroic deed. No, it's perfect love that wipes out fear. Fortitude is what we have to rely on, have to call on, until we reach the point where our ability to love God erases all our fears.

The saints come close to that while on earth. They, more than the rest of us, are less likely to be shaken by what's thrown at them or what might be thrown at them. But then there really is no "them" and "us." We're all called to become saints. To love God wholeheartedly. We all have that potential.

Even perfect human love—the love Jesus had for the Father—doesn't mean a stoicism that is indifferent to pain or welcomes death for its own sake. In the garden of Gethsemane, Christ prayed, "My Father, if it is possible, let this cup pass from me; yet not what I want but what you want" (Matthew 26:39).

Christian martyrs from apostolic times down to our own age weren't masochists. They weren't numb; they weren't foolhardy; they weren't suicidal. Rather, each had the ability to see, using the eyes of faith, beyond the grave. Each was convinced remaining faithful to God was more important than remaining alive. Each believed mortal death could be the gateway to life eternal.

But what does all this mean for us today? Yes, the line of martyrs continues. Each year priests, religious, and laypeople are put to death because they are Catholic. Few of us will be asked to die that way. All of us are asked to live that way.

What way? To be brave. To be the light put on the stand, not hidden under the basket (Matthew 5:15). At home, in the neighborhood, in the parish, in the community, we're asked to shine. To be willing to appear the fool—the true fool for Christ—by living out what we, in our hearts, say we believe.

That's always risky business. The odds are that no one is going to throw us in prison. No one is going to beat us. No one is going to demand our death. Our risks are much smaller, but that doesn't mean they aren't real, and it doesn't mean they don't concern us. It doesn't mean they don't stop us from doing what we know is right.

Ninety-nine times out of a hundred it's easy to know the right thing to do. (That one-hundredth time we rely heavily on prudence to help us.) What's hard, the majority of those ninety-nine times, is *doing* the right thing. Sometimes it's laziness that keeps us from acting. Sometimes it's pride that keeps us from refraining to act. Many times it's lack of courage that stops us from doing either.

We know we should speak up and defend a colleague who's being trashed by others, but we fear they will then turn on us. (Shades of high school!)

Conversely, we pipe in with a juicy bit of gossip or a clever slam to avoid being considered a Goody Two-shoes (or to show how skillful we are with words).

It can take courage to speak up; it can take courage to shut up. Neither act is earth-shaking. Day to day, our acts of fortitude are small, but they are necessary if we want to be courageous. Why? Because being courageous has to involve doing.

The more we act courageously in small matters, the more likely we are to respond that way in large ones. It's the same with all the virtues. If we don't show acts of kindness on a daily basis, we're not likely to do so when asked to help someone on a larger scale. When, in a large way, are we asked to show Christian courage? When a loved one is seriously ill. When our child has a disability. When our marriage ends or our job is lost. When addiction has us in its merciless grip or we've been the victim of violence. Then to respond in faith, we must respond with fortitude. To face that challenge, to step forward to meet that challenge, and to overcome that challenge to the best of our ability take courage.

And, as we all know, that type of conflict isn't a single, simple battle. It's a war that's fought over time on many fronts. It's one that asks us to give more than we think we can give. That forces us to examine our weaknesses and ask for help from others and from God. That makes us admit, in so many ways, that we aren't in control, and we hate doing that.

Mark Twain is credited with saying that the only things sure in life are death and taxes. But there's another certainty. At some point, in some way, we each face our own hard times, our own personal trial. When we do, we have to choose if we're going to remain loyal to God or abandon our faith.

We Christians pray about that, often unaware that this is what our words mean. In the Lord's Prayer, the Our Father, we say "Lead us not into temptation." Scripture scholars tell us a more accurate translation would be "Do not subject us to the test"; that is, when those hard times come, help us remain faithful. Don't let us be tested beyond what we are able to endure.

This was Jesus' prayer to the Father on the night before he died. Each of us, in one way or another, prays the same prayer because each of us faces his or her own crucifixion. We are asking that, when that time comes and in whatever form it might take, we don't abandon God. That, because of what we have to face, we don't give up what we believe. That the Father gives us what we need to make it through that time.

We're asking for the courage to remain faithful when we're so profoundly frightened. Like Jesus, we're asking that "this cup"—our own personal cup—be taken away. And, like Jesus, we're being asked to accept the Father's will rather than our own. We're asked to trust him.

What can we expect if we do? "Then an angel from heaven appeared to him [Jesus] and gave him strength" (Luke 22:43). Whatever test we're asked to face, we will receive the heavenly strength we need to do just that. God has not abandoned us. He never will.

Ultimately, that's what Christian courage is. It's offering ourselves to God and realizing—though we may not see how or may, at times, find it hard to believe—that he will triumph. And with him, so will we.

To Read More about It

Catherine de Hueck Doherty, *Poustinia: Christian Spirituality of the East for Western Man* (Notre Dame, Ind.: Ave Maria Press, 1975).

Maximilian M. Kolbe, *The Kolbe Reader* (Libertyville, Ill.: Franciscan Marytown Press, 1987).

Patricia Treece, *A Man for Others: Maximilian Kolbe, Saint of Auschwitz, in the Words of Those Who Knew Him* (San Francisco: Harper and Row, 1982).

Marina Warner, *Joan of Arc: The Image of Female Heroism* (New York: Alfred A. Knopf, 1981).

Temperance

In One Life

Possibly no other contemporary Catholic author is more widely read and written about than Thomas Merton. His autobiography, *The Seven Storey Mountain,* has touched countless lives since it was first published in 1948.

It's a story reminiscent of the lives of other prominent figures in the church who had towering intellects. A search for what matters most in life ends with (or, it might be argued, begins with) the conclusion that the answer lies in moving toward the life to come, in stripping away the world to better recognize eternity.

Merton was born in Prades, France, on January 31, 1915. His parents, Owen and Ruth, were both artists; his father was from

New Zealand, his mother from America. When he was a year and a half old, the family moved to the United States, and, in 1918, his brother, John Paul, was born.

Two years later, Ruth became terminally ill with stomach cancer. After she died in 1921, Owen often left the two boys in the care of their maternal grandparents while he pursued his artistic career. Later Thomas was sent to boarding schools in France and England, where formal religious practices became a part of his life for the first time, including grace before meals, Sunday worship in the nearby parish church, and kneeling to say bedtime prayers. He would later refer to this period as his "religious phase." It didn't last.

Although Owen tried, he was unable to bring the fractured little family together again before he, too, died of cancer. Thomas was two weeks shy of his sixteenth birthday when he became an orphan. He was placed under the guardianship of his godfather, a London physician who had been a friend of his father. Money from a life-insurance endowment Owen had set up provided enough income for both sons for the near future. Thomas continued living at the boarding school he had been attending, a place where he had gained a reputation for his intellectual power. He planned a diplomatic career but also spoke of writing.

His father's death was painful for him, of course, but it also gave Thomas a new sense of freedom. "Of license" might be a better description. His guardian held some influence over his lifestyle, but not much. Thomas completed his studies at the boarding school (equivalent to finishing high school) at the end of 1932. The next month, his godfather gave him tickets for a vacation in Rome. There, much to his surprise, he was moved by the beauty and symbolism of Byzantine mosaics in Christian churches. He bought a Latin edition of the Bible and began to read it.

But, again, his fervor quickly faded. By the time he entered Clare College of Cambridge University that fall, he was once again the brilliant, open-to-any-immediate-pleasure Thomas Merton. "I was breaking my neck trying to get everything out of life that you think you can get out of it when you are eighteen," he recalled in *The Seven Storey Mountain.*

"I was stamping the last remains of spiritual vitality out of my soul, and trying with all my might to crush and obliterate the image of the divine liberty that had been implanted in me by God," he noted. "With every nerve and fibre of my being I was laboring to enslave myself in the bonds of my own intolerable disgust."

The "greatest grace . . . that I got out of Cambridge" was the study of Dante's poem *The*

Divine Comedy, he wrote. In fact, the Italian poet's vivid description of purgatory's mountain of seven stories would later give Merton the title of his autobiography.

But at the same time, "I, whose chief trouble was that my soul and all its faculties were going to seed because there was nothing to control my appetites—and they were pouring themselves out in an incoherent riot of undirected passion—came to the conclusion that the cause of all my unhappiness was sex-repression!"

He knew the cure for that.

Before the year was over, his lack of discipline, shown in too many nights spent carousing and drinking instead of studying, led to his getting a young woman pregnant. His guardian arranged for her and the baby's care and then, weary of calling Thomas on the carpet for misdeeds, washed his hands of his godson. (There were rumors both mother and child died in the World War II blitz. As late as 1944, Merton thought they were alive. That year, his will stipulated that half his estate should go to his godfather to be passed on "to the person mentioned to him in my letters, if that person can be contacted.")

"It did not take very much reflection on the year I had spent at Cambridge to show me that all my dreams of fantastic pleasures and delights were crazy and absurd," he wrote, "and that everything I had reached out for had turned to ashes in my hands, and that I myself, into the bargain, had turned out to be an extremely unpleasant sort of person—vain, self-centered, dissolute, weak, irresolute, undisciplined, sensual, obscene and proud. I was a mess."

He had equally harsh words for "materialistic society," which "has produced what seems to be the ultimate limit of this worldliness." Nowhere, except perhaps pagan Rome, "has there ever been such a flowering of cheap and petty and disgusting lusts and vanities as in the world of capitalism," he added, "where there is no evil that is not fostered and encouraged for the sake of making money."

Thomas then moved back to the United States and began attending Columbia University, where he received a bachelor's degree in literature and poetry in 1937 (and a master's in 1939). During those years, he dabbled with communism but was unimpressed with its advocates because "nobody was very enthusiastic about getting something to drink except me."

On the other hand, reading *The Spirit of Medieval Philosophy* by Etienne Gilson helped him discover that "the Catholic conception of God was something tremendously solid." Aldous Huxley's *Ends and Means* really threw him for a loop. The point of the title, Merton wrote, was that "we cannot use evil means to attain a good end." Huxley "traced our impossibility to use the proper means to the fact that men were immersed in the material and animal urges of an element of their nature which was blind and crude and unspiritual."

What truly shocked Merton was Huxley's belief that to overcome "this more or less inferior element" and "reassert the dominance of our mind and will . . . we must practice prayer and asceticism."

"Asceticism!" Merton gasped. "The very thought of such a thing was a complete revolution in my mind. The word had so far stood for a kind of weird and ugly perversion of nature, the masochism of men who had gone crazy in a warped and unjust society."

He confessed that "to deny the desires of one's flesh, and even to practice certain disciplines that punished and mortified those desires . . . had never succeeded in giving me anything but gooseflesh." Huxley was proposing that "this negation is not something absolute, sought for its own sake." Rather, "it was a freeing, a vindication of our real selves." In Merton's opinion, Huxley leaned a bit too far toward "the old Protestant groove" of "heresies that make the material creation evil itself."

Still, he wrote, "my own personal misery . . . and the general crisis of the world [teetering on the brink of yet another global war] made me accept with my whole heart this revelation of the need for a spiritual life, an interior life, including some kind of mortification." Merton liked the theory, anyway. But he was more inclined to apply it to himself in areas that didn't much need it — anger and hatred — while, at the same time, "neglecting the ones that really needed to be checked, like gluttony and lust."

He found himself becoming more the Christian apologist, the defender of Christian thought, "all the while stoking the fires of the argument with Scotch and soda." He visited Catholic churches and even went so far (and it was going far, to his way of thinking) as attending a Mass. During this period, his reading became more Catholic until, in 1938, he was baptized.

"The truth is, after receiving the immense grace of Baptism," he wrote, "after all the struggles of persuasion and conversion, and after all the long way I had come, through so much of the no-man's land that lies around the confines of hell, instead of becoming a strong and ardent and generous Catholic, I simply slipped into the ranks of the millions of tepid and dull and sluggish and indifferent Christians who live a life that is still half animal and who barely put up a struggle to keep the breath of grace alive in their souls."

At age twenty-three, Merton didn't realize ("it never occurred to me") that if he continued to live as he had been living, he "would be simply incapable of avoiding mortal sin." Before being baptized, he "lived for myself alone. I had lived for the satisfaction of my own desires and ambitions, for pleasure and comfort and reputation and success." But baptism "had brought with it the obligation to reduce my natural appetites to subordination to God's will."

But, he noted, quoting Scripture, "the wisdom of the flesh is an enemy of God: for it is not subject to the law of God, neither can it be. And they who are in the flesh, cannot please God . . . and if you live according to the flesh, you shall die: but if by the Spirit you mortify the deeds of the flesh, you shall live. For whoever are led by the Spirit of God, they are the sons of God" (Romans 8:7–8, 13–14).

In 1941, Merton entered the Trappist Abbey of Our Lady of Gethsemani near Bardstown, Kentucky. He was ordained in 1949 and also served there as master of novices. After the publication of *The Seven Storey Mountain*, Merton's life became a strange, and certainly trying, mix of being a cloistered monk and an internationally known author—a person who craved solitude and contemplation but one whose advice and friendship were sought by prominent Catholic intellectuals and "everyday" folk.

He continued to write poems as well as study and write about spirituality and mysticism. And, as he matured, he admitted he would have said things differently if he had written his autobiography later in life.

Seeking greater solitude, Merton asked and was given permission to live alone as a hermit in a small house on the abbey grounds. It was at that point in his life, in 1966, that he went to a hospital in Louisville for spinal surgery. There he met a student nurse, and they fell in love. One Merton biographer, a fellow Trappist, has noted "there was never anything sexual, in the sense of genital expression, in Tom and Marge's relationship." A few months later, the abbot learned of what was happening and ordered Merton to end it. He did.

In 1968, he was given permission to tour Asia to study Eastern spirituality and meet religious leaders. While in Bangkok, he died by accidental electrocution while bathing.

The previous year, in letters to Catholic Worker cofounder Dorothy Day, Merton had written about temperance and asceticism: "Yes, Lent is a joy," he said of the upcoming liturgical season. "And we do not have to be worried about relishing the cleanness of it. It feels better not to be stuffed. A little emptiness does one good, and I think it is better now that it is something one can choose without any sense of legal obligation. More of a gift. Not that I'm a strict ascetic myself, I assure you. Far from it."

And in late summer: "The hermit life is no joke at all, and no picnic, but in it one gradually comes face to face with the awful need of self-emptying and even of a kind of annihilation so that God may be all."

In the end, Merton's words echoed those of another rich, pleasure-seeking young man who gave it all up as he discovered the path to true happiness. Seven centuries earlier, it was St. Francis of Assisi who prayed, "It is in dying that we are born to eternal life."

Merton spent his life finding the same truth, the same God.

In Scripture

Scripture is packed with references to faith, hope, and love. It's easy to find prudence, justice, and fortitude, too. But passages on temperance are relatively rare.

These days we might associate this virtue with abstaining from alcohol, especially the temperance movement that led to Prohibition in the early part of the twentieth century. But temperance is broader than that. By definition, it's habitual moderation in the indulgence of the appetites or passions. It's never going hog-wild.

Not eating too much or too little, not sleeping too much or too little, and so on.

Temperance might be called the Goldilocks virtue. It's living "just right."

Compared to the theological virtues and prudence, justice, and fortitude, only a handful of passages from Scripture mention temperance (or moderation, forbearance, and self-control). Maybe the most notable is one that lists the four virtues touted by Plato, the ones we call "cardinal": "And if anyone loves righteousness, her [wisdom's] labors are virtues; for she teaches self-control and prudence, justice and courage" (Wisdom 8:7).

The book of Proverbs offers advice on the temperate life (25:16–17, 28): Don't eat too much honey or you'll get sick to your stomach. Don't hang around at the neighbors' house too frequently or they'll get tired of you. And "like a city breached, without walls, is one who lacks self-control."

Sirach gives the same message (18:30–19:3). If you "follow your base desires" and don't "restrain your appetites," you'll end up "the laughingstock of your enemies." If you're a temperate person, you don't "revel in great luxury, or you may become impoverished by its expense." You don't "become a beggar by feasting with borrowed money, when you have nothing in your purse." (This was thousands of years before the first credit card!)

The one who drinks too much does not become rich, Sirach notes. The one who doesn't pay attention to the little things fails "little by little" (19:1). "Wine and women lead intelligent men astray." (And, it certainly seems safe to flip that passage to read "Wine and men lead intelligent women astray.") The person who "consorts with prostitutes is reckless," and "decay and worms will take possession" of him or her. Indeed, "the reckless person"—the one who is intemperate—"will be snatched away" (19:2–3).

Sirach 31:12–24 describes proper banquet etiquette. (Don't be greedy. Don't grab everything you see. Don't "crowd your neighbor at the dish.") "How ample a little is for a well-disciplined person!" Sirach notes. That person sleeps more soundly ("healthy sleep depends on moderate eating") and wakes up early, feeling refreshed. In contrast, "the distress of sleeplessness and of nausea and colic are with the glutton." So temperance is healthy: "In everything you do be moderate, and no sickness will overtake you."

All this is followed by advice on drinking alcohol (31:25–31).

Among the book's observations: "Wine is very life to human beings if taken in moderation" and "Wine drunk at the proper time and in moderation is rejoicing of heart and gladness of soul."

And among its warnings: "Do not try to prove your strength by wine-drinking, for wine has destroyed many" and "Wine drunk to excess leads to bitterness of spirit, to quarrels and stumbling."

But how much is too much? That varies from person to person, and we each have to know our own limits. "My child," Sirach advises, "test yourself while you live; see what is bad for you and do not give in to it. For not everything is good for everyone, and no one enjoys everything" (37:27–28).

Then, repeating what he has taught earlier, he adds: "Do not be greedy for every delicacy, and do not eat without restraint; for overeating brings sickness, and gluttony leads to nausea. Many have died of gluttony, but the one who guards against it prolongs his life" (37:29–31).

In the New Testament, we find Paul, while being held in custody, discussing "justice, self-control, and the coming judgment" (Acts 24:25) with his captor, Felix (the governor of Judea from 52 to 60). Paul's words frightened Felix. The apostle wrote about temperance in his letters to the various communities of the early church. What he had to say wasn't just about food and drink but also sex. Apparently some married residents of Corinth had taken the advice he had given celibates and were applying it too strictly in their own lives. Though properly wed, they were refraining from sexual relations.

"Do not deprive one another except perhaps by agreement for a set time, to devote yourselves to prayer," he told them, "and then come together again, so that Satan may not tempt you because of your lack of self-control" (1 Corinthians 7:5).

"This I say by way of concession, not of command," he added. "I wish that all were as I myself am [that is, celibate]. But each has a particular gift from God, one having one kind and another a different kind" (7:6–7). In addition, those unmarried and widowed who "are not practicing self-control" should find a spouse because "it is better to marry than to be aflame with passion" (7:9). *Aflame* doesn't refer to the fires of hell but to the torturous struggle of remaining celibate.

A little later in the same letter, Paul talks about temperance and the way an athlete trains. "Do you not know that in a race the runners all compete, but only one receives the prize? Run in such a way that you may win it. Athletes exercise self-control in all things; they do it to receive a perishable wreath, but we an imperishable one. So I do not run aimlessly, nor do I box as though beating the air; but I punish my body and enslave it, so that after proclaiming to others I myself should not be disqualified" (9:24–27).

Temperance—self-control, self-restraint—is the virtue that builds spiritual strength. The one that allows us to "win." And it, Paul says, comes from the Holy Spirit. "The fruit of Spirit is love, joy, peace, patience, kindness, generosity, faithfulness, gentleness, and self-control" (Galatians 5:22–23).

In another letter, he tells Timothy to be brave in his ministry because, with ordination, "God did not give us a spirit of cowardice, but rather a spirit of power and of love and of self-discipline" (2 Timothy 1:7).

In 2 Peter, the author describes how temperance is a link in the chain of virtues that is a Christian lifestyle. God has promised us heaven, and "for this very reason, you must make every effort to support your faith with goodness, and goodness with knowledge, and knowledge with self-control, and self-control with endurance, and endurance with godliness, and godliness with mutual affection, and mutual affection with love. For if these things are yours and are increasing among you, they keep you from being ineffective and unfruitful in the knowledge of our Lord Jesus Christ" (2 Peter 1:5–8). And, "in this way," through practicing these virtues, "entry into the eternal kingdom of our Lord and Savior Jesus Christ will be richly provided for you" (2 Peter 1:11).

Down through the Ages

"Restraint, meekness, chastity, steadfastness, patience and similar great virtues are given us by God for weapons to resist and oppose the tribulations we meet with, and to help us when they occur," St. Antony of Egypt wrote in a work called *170 Texts on Saintly Life.* Antony was an Egyptian monk who lived from the middle of the third century to the middle of the fourth. The communities he established became models for monastic life, especially in the East.

"So if we train ourselves in the use of these powers," he wrote, "and keep them always ready, then nothing that can befall us will ever be hard, grievous, destructive or unbearable, for all would be overcome by the virtues we possess."

Antony wrote a great deal about "intelligent" people, and by that he meant "not those who have studied the sayings and writings of the wise men of old, but those whose soul is intelligent, who can judge what is good and what evil." An intelligent person is a temperate person because "the more a man uses moderation in his life, the more he is at peace, for he is not full of cares for many things—servants, hired laborers and acquisition of cattle."

When we "cling to such things," Antony said, "we become liable to vexations arising from them and are led to murmur against God." (We complicate our lives and then get mad at God because our lives are complicated.) "Thus our self-willed desire (for many things) fills us with turmoil and we wander in the darkness of a sinful life, not knowing ourselves."

And we can't use the excuse that *everybody* wants lots of things. People who are "simple and uneducated . . . laugh at sciences and refuse to hear anything about them, for knowledge shows up their ignorance — and they want everyone to be like them." In the same way, those "of unrestrained life and character greatly desire all to be worse than themselves, thinking to find themselves excused by the fact that the wicked are many."

It's the old "I'm not so bad compared to him" or "She's a lot worse than I am." If we live that way, then desires — for food, drink, sex, power, money — are holding us captive. "Regard as free not those who are free by their status [we might think of the wealthy who can have "everything"] but those who are free in their life and disposition. For example, one should not call truly free people who are illustrious and rich when they are wicked and intemperate, for such men are slaves of sensual passions."

No, "freedom and blessedness of the soul are the result of true purity and contempt for temporal things." It's "those whose life is passed in small and modest efforts [who] become free of dangers and have no need of special precautions. By always conquering desires, they readily find the way leading to God."

We've all heard this before. But, Antony points out, "those who are beguiled by earthly blessings, while knowing to the last word all that should be done to lead a good life, resemble those who have acquired remedies and medical appliances, but do not know how to use them and do not even trouble about it."

We know what temperance is. The hard part is applying that knowledge in our everyday lives. How to do it? "At the uprising of each of the passions of your soul, remember that those who think rightly and wish to put what concerns them . . . on a right and firm foundation, count as delight not the acquiring of perishable riches, but true glory (in heaven). . . . Those who reason in this way are not enticed by the illusory glitter of riches and other delights."

It's better, Antony taught, to think of those earthly "delights" (whatever they might be) as something that will trip us up. "As excessively long garments hinder travelers in their walking, so desire for excessive possessions does not allow the soul to make efforts and be saved." The choice is ours. "If you wish, you can be a slave of passions, and if you wish, you can remain free and not submit to their yoke; for God has created you with that power."

Antony admits temperance is a lifelong struggle that has to be fought on many fronts. "Those who take part in Olympic games are not crowned after defeating one, or another, or a third opponent, but after defeating them all. In the same way every man who wishes to be crowned by God must teach his soul chastity [that is, proper self-control], not only in relation to bodily passions, but also when he is tempted by greed of gain, by desire to seize what does not belong to him, by envy, by love of pleasure, vainglory . . . and the like."

The monk wrote, "Souls not bridled by reason and not governed by a mind which restrains, steadies and directs (correctly) their passions—i.e. pleasure and pain—perish like dumb beasts, for their reason is swept along by passions, like a driver by runaway horses."

Some seven centuries after St. Antony, German mystic Hildegard of Bingen (1098–1179) used equally striking images in *The Book of Rewards of Life*. In it she describes a series of visions she had that portrayed both virtues and vices.

"Immoderation," she wrote, was "a wolf who crouched down. He watched carefully so that he might gulp down anything he could snatch."

The wolf said, "'Whatever I want to seek, I will snatch. I will hold nothing back from myself. Why should I hold anything back from myself and then have no reward?'"

Hildegard wrote, "Again I heard a voice from the storm clouds answer this image, saying, 'O watcher of snares, with your snares you bite into all the things that are honest and rational since you are like a young animal who knows no moderation; you act like an unclean animal. . . . You . . . are maimed with disease and are like a cadaver full of worms.'" Strong words from a prim and proper nun!

"When a man rebels against the good things of God," Hildegard said, "immoderation shoots up everywhere it is able. . . . The image is like a wolf because without discretion, man has the madness of deceit and the rough changeableness of evil. He crouches down and watches carefully so that he might gulp down anything he can catch. This means that bent by his own strength, man leans toward the lower part of the worst ways of his own will."

Intemperance can blind us, Hildegard said, and then we put the blame on our human nature. "When a man walks crookedly in luxury through the taste of the flesh, he makes an offering to the devil. For when he is moved to do evil works through taste, he covers the eyes of his soul from knowing good, as if he were covering his eyes with his hands. As a result, he rushes into the darkness with his evil works saying: 'I am not able to stand up, as if I were not made of flesh. For I live from food and drink, as God made me, and therefore, I cannot hold myself back from works of this type.'"

In a letter written to an early Jesuit community, St. Ignatius of Loyola (1491–1556) offered advice on how to live a life of temperance. "Experience shows that such contentment, as it is possible to attain in this life, is found not in those who are negligent, but in the fervent in the service of God," he said. "And naturally so; for by endeavoring to overcome themselves, and to destroy self-love, they dig up with it the roots of the passions and all troubles, while by acquiring habits of virtue, they come naturally to act with ease and joy in conformity to them."

We will be at peace with ourselves in this world to the extent that we replace selfishness with self-control and make virtue our lifestyle.

But, he added, that doesn't mean "what I have so far said to awaken those that may be sleeping, and to spur those who may be lagging or loitering along the road, must not be so understood as to constitute a plea for falling into the opposite extreme of indiscreet fervor." Even with regard to our spiritual life, and maybe especially with regard to it, prudence is finding the middle path. Temperance is following it.

"For spiritual sickness proceeds not only from chilling causes such as tepidity," the founder of the Society of Jesus wrote, "but also from heated causes, such as excessive fervor." (Back to Goldilocks: This way of personal spirituality is too cold, this way is too hot, and this way is just right.)

"As St. Bernard says: The enemy [Satan] has no more efficacious means of depriving the heart of true charity, than by inducing to practice it incautiously and not in accordance with spiritual reasonableness." We've all witnessed the intemperate do-gooder who goes overboard, eventually turning into a snarling bear before giving up entirely.

"When that moderation is not observed," Ignatius told his priests and brothers, "good is turned into evil and virtue into vice; and thence follow many difficulties quite contrary to the intention of the overzealous persons."

What kind of difficulties? "The first is one cannot serve God very long." Burnout. "The second is that what is gained with too much precipitation is often not preserved." The classic house built on sand. "The third is that thus no care is taken to avoid overloading the vessel." We become what we would call "swamped."

"With that excess, as St. Bernard says, four things are lost: efficiency to the body, devotion to the spirit, example to neighbor and honor to God."

Ignatius reminds the community that St. Bernard "concludes that whoever thus ill-treats the living temple of God is sacrilegious and guilty of all that I have said." And each of us is compelled "in all this matter to use discretion, moderating the practice of virtue between the two extremes. . . . So that he who desires to be good to others should not be bad to himself: 'If one is mean to himself, to whom will he be generous?'" (Sirach 14:5).

For Us Today

The British author Oscar Wilde wrote, "I can resist everything except temptation." That's the problem with temperance. It's easy to practice self-control except for when it's time to practice self-control.

Moderation in the abstract makes perfect sense. In the concrete . . . well, couldn't an exception be made just this one time?

That, of course, is the diabolical cleverness of intemperance, of immoderation. Let's be blunt: of greed. We want something and we want it *right now!* But we're not saying we want it all. We're not pigs. No, we just want one more.

One more drink. One more helping of mashed potatoes and gravy. One more hour of sleep. One more hand of cards. One more computer or stereo upgrade. What's the harm? It's just one more. It's just one tiny step from here to there. It's practically nothing.

But, typically, that's where temperance begins. It starts as practically nothing.

We like to think of this virtue as it was demonstrated by Mother Teresa or Mahatma Gandhi. We imagine ourselves in our own sandals and sari, whatever forms they might take. "Look how simply I live! Look how much self-control I have! Look at my amazing humility!"

It would be better to consider those two as the triathletes of temperance, the iron ones who can swim, bike, and run for miles and miles and miles. We know an athlete doesn't start at that level. No, he or she begins at such an easy pace and with such a modest goal that it seems ridiculous.

Strength and stamina are built up over time. Step by step. That's how it is with temperance. It's no wonder so many New Year's resolutions quickly turn to an embarrassing memory, if they're recalled at all. "Starting January 1, I'm going to quit smoking and exercise half an hour every day and lose twenty-five pounds and watch less television and. . . . " We're like the novice jogger who attempts too much his or her first time out and wakes up the next morning barely able to walk.

Ironically, or maybe not surprisingly, the key to becoming more temperate is to work on that virtue temperately. To wade in rather than jump in. That makes sense because moderation is nothing more and nothing less than all those pesky, tiny steps that move us from selfishness to self-control. If we don't exercise moderation in small matters, it's unlikely we will in large ones. And, truth be told, life seldom presents large ones.

In many ways, that's what being a Christian is. Jesus didn't ask everyone he met to immediately go sell everything they had and follow him. He did ask them all to demonstrate a basic concern, a love, for others. How were they to show it? How were they to live it? That was what they had to figure out, through prayer. That was why they needed wisdom.

It's why we do, too. When it comes to temperance, no one can tell us "Here is the definitive line between moderate and immoderate." We each have our own lines, and, to make all this more challenging, that line is not constant. It moves.

Let's use an extreme example. For the man who has smoked three packs of cigarettes a day for twenty years, cutting back to two packs is a hefty bit of temperance. On the other hand, a woman who has smoked one pack a day for a long time is hardly demonstrating moderation if she suddenly starts puffing away at twice that rate. So is smoking two packs a day an act of self-control? Yes. And no.

The line changes as our lives change. A twenty-year-old has little or no trouble getting by on four hours of sleep one night while the same schedule turns a forty-year-old into a groggy, grumpy mess the next day. A forty-year-old may still be able to enjoy a late snack of cold pizza, but a sixty-year-old might know that's a sure ticket to middle-of-the-night heartburn.

All of this is part of temperance. Knowing our limits. Not falling into the trap of thinking we can do something now just because we used to be able to do it. It's giving up the immediate gratification ("But I really want to stay up and see the end of this movie." "But that leftover pizza looks so good.") in order to benefit in the future. We pay a small price now to avoid a larger price later.

But temperance doesn't mean being glum. Doesn't mean being a self-proclaimed, self-shackled martyr. Doesn't mean becoming a zombie. Just the opposite. There is an insepa-rable link between this virtue and joy, between it and freedom, between it and life.

Moderation sets us free from the tyranny of appetite, the craving for self-satisfaction in whatever form it might take. It sets us free from the commandment that dictates "I am hungry; therefore I must be fed." Self-control doesn't deny that hunger. But it doesn't dwell on it either. It doesn't, to use an old examination-of-conscience term, entertain it.

Temperance pushes appetite aside for a greater good. That might be because wisdom has taught us that an appetite appeased is an appetite that soon comes back roaring for even more. It might be because we know that for us here and now this is the limit, this is the line. And it might be because we have learned there is greater joy in living moderately, in paying attention to that more basic hunger, that spiritual hunger, our search for God.

Temperance aids us in that quest by freeing us from the petty concerns the world offers. We don't have to have the best. We don't have to be known as the brightest. By giving up our pursuit of the material rather than giving in to it, we have more time and energy to go after the eternal. We more easily and more readily see the things of this world for what they truly are: rather meager goods compared to what our Creator offers.

No wonder as we increase in temperance, our ability to pray can likewise grow. No wonder as we say no to ourselves in a healthy and holy way, we can find it more natural to say yes to others. No wonder the more we exercise this virtue, the more we come to appreciate it and, temperately, want it to play a deeper role in our lives. No wonder the difference between self-centeredness and self-control looks more and more like the key to understanding the difference between merely existing and being fully alive.

Our view of temperance shifts. No longer seen as saying no to this, it becomes saying yes to that. Yes to what God wants for us, knowing he wants only the best. At times, that can mean saying no to what we might be tempted to believe is greater holiness.

Somehow we can spot that religious extremism in others more easily than we notice it in ourselves. The medieval Catholics who ran from church to church on Sunday to again and again see the consecrated host elevated seem silly. When we spread ourselves too thin by over-volunteering (no matter how admirable the causes) or placing extreme ascetic demands on ourselves, we tend to want to push forward despite the costs. We work hard at convincing ourselves and those around us that the greater the pain, the greater the gain. Hardly a Christian philosophy.

Life is a marathon, not a sprint. The immoderate may win a lap or two, but it's the temperate who stay in the race. With the help of God's grace, they may increase their pace (and, at some points in their life, may need to decrease it), but they will not meet with success if they ignore the natural (or perhaps we could say supernatural) rhythm that fits only them.

Temperance is that little virtue that constantly makes seemingly insignificant demands on us. But, like the rudder on a great ship, it directs our lives.

To Read More about It

Hildegard of Bingen, *Mystical Writings* (New York: Crossroad, 1992).

J. Ignacio Tellechea Idígoras, *Ignatius of Loyola: The Pilgrim Saint* (Chicago: Loyola University Press, 1994).

Ignatius of Loyola, *Letters of St. Ignatius of Loyola,* trans. William J. Young, S.J. (Chicago: Loyola University Press, 1959).

Thomas Merton, *The Seven Storey Mountain* (New York: Harcourt Brace Jovanovich, 1978).

M. Basil Pennington, O.C.S.O., *Thomas Merton: Brother Monk* (San Francisco: Harper and Row, 1987).

Choosing to Grow

The first chapter of this book warned this wasn't a get-spiritually-fit-quick scheme. Examining the theological and cardinal virtues can make it easier to see how we can apply them in our daily lives, but it doesn't necessarily make that application any easier.

"Where virtue is, there are many snares," St. John Chrysostom wrote in the fourth century. For each virtue, there may be several vices, several tempting side paths, that—again, step by step—can lead us off the track.

At times we may become discouraged because we can't see that we're making any progress. At times we may get tired of trying because the unvirtuous seem to be so richly rewarded. At times we may feel empty or lost, frightened or numb.

There can be a long period between the planting of a seed and the harvesting of a crop. But each day of sunshine, each rainfall, each bit of nutrient in the soil (and sometimes not a little fertilizer) are necessary for that seed of possibility to reach its full potential and bear fruit.

We're the same. "Virtue is a gift from God implanted in our nature," St. John Damsacene wrote in the eighth century. Today may be sunny; tonight, bitter cold. Some days we may easily draw sustenance from prayer and from those we love. Other days our life, our future, perhaps our very soul, may seem overwhelmed by . . . fertilizer.

Through it all, unlike the common garden seed, we have a choice. We have to make a choice. Spiritual growth doesn't just happen. Relying on God's infinite goodness and grace, we play a part in making it happen. Unlike the ordinary seed, we must choose to grow. Choose to blossom. Choose to bear fruit.

We must choose virtue.

Why? Because it leads us to the only One who can calm our restless heart. It leads us home.

Sources

Walter M. Abbott, S.J., ed., *The Documents of Vatican II* (New York: Guild Press, 1966).

Aelred of Rievaulx, *Mirror of Charity* (Kalamazoo, Mich.: Cistercian Publications, 1990).

Ambrose, "Isaac, or the Soul" in *The Fathers of the Church* (Washington, D.C.: Catholic University of America Press, 1971).

Anselm, *Basic Writings: Proslogium, Monologium, Cur Deus Homo,* and *Gaunilon's on Behalf of the Fool,* trans. S. N. Deane (LaSalle, Ill.: Open Court, 1962).

Antony the Great, *170 Texts on Saintly Life* in *Early Fathers from the Philokalia* (London: Faber and Faber, 1969).

Thomas Aquinas, *Summa Theologiae* (New York: Benziger Brothers, 1946).

Augustine, *The Confessions of St. Augustine* (Garden City, N.Y.: Doubleday, 1960).

Augustine, "Faith, Hope and Charity (Enchiridion de fide, spe et caritate)" in *The Fathers of the Church,* trans. Bernard M. Peebles (New York: CIMA Publishing, 1947).

Basil, "On Mercy and Justice" in *Fathers of the Church* (New York: Fathers of the Church, Inc., 1950).

Alban Butler, *Butler's Lives of the Saints* (New York: P. J. Kenedy and Sons, 1956).

John Cassian, "The Conferences of John Cassian" in *A Select Library of Nicene and Post-Nicene Fathers of the Christian Church,* Philip Schaff and Henry Wace, eds. (Grand Rapids, Mich.: Eerdmans, 1973).

Catechism of the Catholic Church (Liguori, Mo.: Liguori Publications, 1994).

Romanus Cessario, O.P., *The Moral Virtues and Theological Ethics* (Notre Dame, Ind.: University of Notre Dame Press, 1991).

Cyprian, *The Epistles of Cyprian* (The Holy Bible Web Site: http://www.redbay.com/newbies /mag).

Dorothy Day, *From Union Square to Rome* (Silver Spring, Md.: Preservation of the Faith Press, 1940).

Dorothy Day, *The Long Loneliness: An Autobiography* (San Francisco: Harper and Row, 1981).

Dorothy Day, *Meditations* (New York: Newman Press, 1970).

Catherine de Hueck Doherty, *Poustinia: Christian Spirituality of the East for Western Man* (Notre Dame, Ind.: Ave Maria Press, 1975).

Avery Dulles, S.J., *The Assurance of Things Hoped For: A Theology of Christian Faith* (New York and Oxford: Oxford University Press, 1994).

Eknath Easwaran, *Seeing with the Eyes of Love: Reflections on a Classic of Christian Mysticism* (Tomales, Calif.: Nilgiri Press, 1991).

Jim Forest, *Living With Wisdom: A Life of Thomas Merton* (Maryknoll, N.Y.: Orbis, 1991).

Gregory I, *Pastoral Care*, trans. Henry Davis, S.J., in *Ancient Christian Writers: The Works of the Fathers in Translation* (New York: Newman Press, 1979).

Hildegard of Bingen, *The Book of the Rewards of Life* (*Liber Vitae Meritorum*) (New York: Garland Publishing, 1994).

Hildegard of Bingen, *Mystical Writings* (New York: Crossroad, 1992).

Ignatius of Antioch, "The Epistle of Ignatius to the Ephesians" in *The Ante-Nicene Father*, vol. 1., pp. 45–58 (Grand Rapids, Mich.: Eerdmans, 1981).

Ignatius of Loyola, *Letters and Instructions of St. Ignatius Loyola* (St. Louis, Mo.: B. Herder, 1914).

Ignatius of Loyola, *Letters of St. Ignatius of Loyola*, trans. William J. Young, S.J. (Chicago: Loyola University Press, 1959).

John of the Cross, *The Ascent of Mount Carmel* in *The Collected Works of St. John of the Cross*, trans. Kieran Kavanaugh, O.C.D., and Otilio Rodriguez, O.C.D. (Washington, D.C.: ICS Publications, 1973).

John XXIII, *Journal of a Soul* (New York: McGraw-Hill, 1965).

Maximilian M. Kolbe, *Stronger than Hatred: A Collection of Spiritual Writings* (New York: New City Press, 1988).

C. S. Lewis, *Mere Christianity* (New York: Macmillan, 1952).

Martin Luther, "Preface to the Epistle of St. Paul to the Romans" in *Martin Luther: Selections from His Writings* (Garden City, N.Y.: Doubleday, 1961).

Maximus Confessor, "The Four Centuries on Charity" in Johannes Quasten and Joseph C. Plumpe, *Ancient Christian Writers*, trans. Polycarp Sherwood, O.S.B. (Westminster, Md.: Newman Press, 1955).

Lucy Menzies, *St. Margaret Queen of Scotland* (London: J. M. Dent and Sons, Ltd., 1925).

Thomas Merton, *The Hidden Ground of Love* (New York: Farrar, Straus, and Giroux, 1985).

Thomas Merton, *The Seven Storey Mountain* (New York: Harcourt Brace Jovanovich, 1978).

M. Basil Pennington, O.C.S.O., *Thomas Merton: Brother Monk* (San Francisco: Harper and Row, 1987).

Josef Pieper, *A Brief Reader on the Virtues of the Human Heart,* trans. Paul C. Duggan (San Francisco: Ignatius Press, 1991).

Josef Pieper, *The Four Cardinal Virtues* (Notre Dame, Ind.: University of Notre Dame Press, 1966).

Josef Pieper, *On Hope* (San Francisco: Ignatius Press, 1986).

S. Th. Pinckaers and C.-J. Pinto de Oliveira, *Sainte Therese d'Ávila: Contemplation et renouveau de l'Eglise* (Fribourg, Suisse: Editions Universitaires, 1986).

Ingvald Raknem, *Joan of Arc in Legend and Literature* (Oslo: Universitetsforlaget, 1971).

Oscar Romero, *Voice of the Voiceless* (Maryknoll, N.Y.: Orbis Books, 1990).

Teresa of Ávila, *The Book of the Foundations of St. Teresa of Jesus* (London: Thomas Baker, 1913).

Thomas à Kempis, *Imitation of Christ,* trans. Leo Sherley-Price (Baltimore: Penguin, 1968).

Patricia Treece, *A Man for Others: Maximilian Kolbe, Saint of Auschwitz, in the Words of Those Who Knew Him* (San Francisco: Harper and Row, 1982).

Desmond Tutu, *Crying in the Wilderness: The Struggle for Justice in South Africa* (Grand Rapids, Mich.: Eerdmans, 1982).

Desmond Tutu, *Hope and Suffering* (Grand Rapids, Mich.: Eerdmans, 1984).

Marina Warner, *Joan of Arc: The Image of Female Heroism* (New York: Alfred A. Knopf, 1981).

Kenneth L. Woodward, *Making Saints* (New York: Touchstone, 1990).

Also from

Loyola Press

LIVING THE BEATITUDES TODAY
Happily Ever After Begins Here and Now
by Bill Dodds and Michael J. Dodds, O.P.

"We live in a time when it's easy to feel overwhelmed and confused. We live in a time when Jesus' words about being happy can give us reason to hope."
—from *Living the Beatitudes Today*

ISBN: 0-8294-0970-X; $10.95 paperback

THE SEEKER'S GUIDE TO THE CHRISTIAN STORY
by Mitch Finley

"One who would nourish an adult faith must pay attention to the history of the church. For if I know where I come from, if I understand better the roots of my religious tradition, the "stories of the church," I became liberated to face the present and the future with greater confidence, hope and common sense."
—from *The Seeker's Guide to the Christian Story*

ISBN: 0-8294-1020-1; $10.95 paperback

THE SEEKER'S GUIDE TO BEING CATHOLIC
by Mitch Finley

"All Catholics are 'seekers' so this book is good for all of us. But it is particularly good for marginal Catholics, uneasy Catholics, troubled Catholics, borderline Catholics, ex-Catholics who wonder and worry about their ex-ness. It would also be helpful to those who feel attracted to Catholicism, but do not know why."
—Theodore M. Hesburgh, C.S.C.

ISBN: 0-8294-0934-3; $10.95 paperback

Available at your local bookstore or direct from Loyola Press.
Send your check, money order, or VISA/MasterCard information (including $4.50 for shipping one copy, $5.00 for two copies, or $6.50 for three) to:

LOYOLA PRESS, ATTN: CUSTOMER SERVICE, 3441 NORTH ASHLAND, CHICAGO, ILLINOIS 60657   800-621-1008